George's World

The life story of George Bamby,
the UK's number 1 paparazzi photographer

Written by Madison Webbe
in collaboration with George Bamby

Paperback ISBN: 9798771375960

First paperback edition November 2021

Self-published Kindle Direct Publishing

Disclaimer

These are my memories, from my perspective, and I have tried to represent events as faithfully as possible

Dedicated to Lewis Bamby

Apple of dad's eye
Forever in mum's heart

George's World

A CHILDHOOD LOST

What makes us the adults we become? It's the old nature versus nurture argument, the answer to which we will probably never unravel. Well, I know what made me the man I am. I know the defining moment in my life that set me on a track to adulthood with a determination unrivalled amongst any of my peers. There was a moment in my past that arrived, unpredicted, unplanned and with a force so tremendous that it would change the course of my life.

As a boy of 12, on June 14th 1984, I went to stay at my nanna and grandad's house for a couple of nights. As you will later come to understand, I was happy to be staying there and to get away from my mother and stepdad at home.

Looking out of the window, we could see lots of kids playing out in the street and, being boisterous boys of twelve, we were soon itching to go out too. It was quite usual for the children in the area to play in the road and, as we were getting under nanna's feet, when David suggested that we be allowed out, she didn't object.

Racing out of the back door, we joined in with the other lads, kicking about an old football. At first, we played outside nanna's house but then we all wandered off up the street, me and David chatting and laughing as we always did when we were together. He was the nearest thing I had to a brother. Before we knew it, we were a couple of streets away, under an old railway bridge in Thomas Street, which is in the Stretford area of Manchester. We still had the football with us, so we had a bit of a kick-about, shouting and laughing, with not a worry in the world.
Wherever we seemed to be, we were never very far from a chip shop and the smell of vinegar wafted up the street, enticing us like two 'Bisto kids', following their noses in pursuit of a good meal. The 30p I had in my pocket was more than enough to get me and David what was known in the area as a chip barm cake: chips on a buttered round bread roll, and I remember that they cost 12p each. We sat on the pavement outside the chippy, our backs to the window, melted butter running down onto my hands, which I licked off enthusiastically. The barm cakes were satisfying and we laughed as we ate. Gradually all the other lads disappeared off home, leaving me and David to entertain ourselves.

We were kicking the football from one to the other, travelling along the road at the same time, when we saw a gap in the fence and, being the adventurers that we were, we slipped through the hole. We were boys pushing the limits, finding our own excitement and it never even entered our heads that we should not have gone through the fence, and it was just so easy. Climbing up the grass verge on the other side, we found ourselves on a railway line and I felt that tingle of the unknown, that pull to find out the answer to 'what if?', so without any thought for our safety, we started to walk along the line. There's a sort of deserted emptiness about a railway line, but didn't that rail just asked to be walked along? We didn't know it then, but we were at the old Kellogg factory in Trafford Park, and it was all pretty desolate as we kicked our football along.

We walked through a car park, and I saw an old goods carriage on the line in front of us. It didn't take much effort to climb up onto the top of it and I stood there looking down on David and the rest of the world. Suddenly, anything was possible! I was a superhero. After all, hadn't I just climbed Everest?!

I jumped from that carriage to the next.
I could almost fly…
feel that exhilaration!
I'd seen this done in a movie.
I jumped from carriage
to carriage.
Then,
in that instance,
my life
changed
forever.

MY EARLY YEARS

Stretford Memorial Hospital, Manchester, 12th December 1971.

I don't know if my dad was pleased when I arrived on the scene, but I was given his name: George Bamby, so George Bamby II had joined the population. I don't think I must have made much of an entrance as my birth was never talked about. I suppose I caused the same amount of fuss coming into the world as all the other babies in the maternity ward, as I'm sure if my birth had been anything out of the ordinary, I would have been reminded of it later on in my childhood.

Home was on Cooper Street, which was in the middle of a council estate in a rough area of Stretford. At the end of the road was the Corolla Factory, a manufacturing plant for soft drinks, which brought work to many on the estate. I don't know if my mum and dad had been happy before I was born but I know that times were hard. My sister, Victoria, had been born 18 months previous and I had an elder brother, Karl, who was eighteen month's her senior. When I arrived in the world he was already living with my nanna and grandad, so my father couldn't have been much of a family man to allow his three-year-old son to live with someone else. I don't know how much of a decision it took for my mum to leave him there permanently, but the story goes that when she used to go out shopping, she would leave him with nanna and granddad. I was told that when she picked him up, she would pinch him to make him cry so nanna would say to leave him there and I think one day he just ended up staying for good. Maybe they managed with Vicky alright, but I don't suppose for a minute that they were happy when they found out that mum was pregnant again.

Shortly after I was born, my dad left. I don't remember him at all, but I know that he was a turf accountant. In more recent years, my parentage as far as my father was concerned was brought into question, which led onto a completely different chapter of my life and brought me face to face with Charles Bronson, the UK's most notorious and longest-serving prisoner. For the purpose of this book though, I will keep it true to the facts as I understood them at the time of writing.

No-one ever had a good word to say about my father. My mother said that some gangsters had been after him once because when he worked for them as a bookmaker, he had been putting bets through for races that had already run and had pocketed the winnings. She said he changed the clock on the machine to make them look like legitimate bets. Later in life, my grandad told me that, allegedly, dad had tried it on with my mum's sister, Shirley. I don't know how true that was. Maybe grandad just didn't want me to think that he left because I had come into the household. My mother never really talked about him except to say that he was a bastard, and she recounted an incident when money was thin on the ground, the family hadn't eaten for two days and there was no money for the electricity meter. She said that dad got a Mars bar out of his pocket, unwrapped it and tried to eat it without anyone seeing him.

So, my mother became a single parent. I've seen photographs of her from this time and to me she looked like a 'good-time girl'. Allegedly, she went out drinking whenever she could, and she looked and acted tough so that no-one would mess with her. If anyone dared to challenge her, she was not averse to fighting and I recall that she had a scar about the size of a five pence piece on the back of her hand. One night when she was short of money for beer, she bet a couple of guys in the pub that she could put a cigarette out on her hand. She won the bet and they had to pay for her drinks all night. I think that gives an impression of the kind of person that she was then, and she's probably still got a scar there now, a reminder of how much she valued herself and to what lengths she would go to for a drink.

STEPDAD

Some time after I was born, my mother met a man named Arthur Cooper. He soon became my stepdad, when they married, and me and Vicky were given his surname. To the outside world, he was a good man. After all, hadn't he taken on another man's children? Whenever he left the house, he was always smartly dressed with pressed trousers and shirt, polished shoes and combed hair. He had the appearance of a respectable man, but that exterior belied the person beneath.

My first memory of him is quite specific: a day when I was standing in the hallway, near the front door, and my mum was in the living room. She regularly had bad hangovers, so I imagine that on this occasion she was recovering from the night before as I could see her lying on the couch with her feet towards me. My stepdad stood in the doorway shouting at her.
"You lying bitch, you've fucking slept with him!"
I don't think that I really understood at the time what they were arguing about, but they were both shouting.
"You dirty, lying bitch!"
First it was the words, but then when they didn't hurt enough, he threw his red-hot cup of tea over her.

When I was very young, Arthur was a fence erector. Later, I don't remember him ever working, but at that time he put fences up for a living and as he had a friend with a company in Saudi Arabia, he often worked away. I suppose, as a baby, I may have been tolerable to him, especially as he had so many trips out of the country.

When I was two years old, we moved to another council house in Kings Road, Stretford. No. 411. I will always remember it. Quite recently, I drove past and saw a 'For Sale' sign outside. I would love to have bought the property and then I would have knocked it down brick by brick.

About four years later, I recall an instance in time: It's a small but significant memory… Life was about to change once more. My mother was pregnant again and this time the child was to be Arthur's own flesh and blood. The new addition to the family was Kelly and she was the most beautiful thing I had ever seen, and I loved her from the minute I set eyes on her. I thought that she was the best thing that had ever happened to me, and my memory was of me bouncing her on my knee. I thought that the three of us kids would be the best family ever, and forever.

At some point, the pretence of a happy family life must have become too much for my mother though. She loaded all of us kids and a few bags into a taxi and we went to my Auntie's house. My mum's sister, Shirley, lived in the next road to our old house in Cooper Street. I think we were all oblivious to the anxiety that my mum must have felt. Just as the taxi was pulling away, Arthur's car drove up behind us and he followed until we stopped outside Shirley's house. Auntie Shirley rushed out and the two women, like lionesses protecting their cubs, ushered us all inside and shut the door.
"Don't speak to him" Shirley was saying.
Arthur started hammering on the door.
"Don't' let him in, Carol!"
"He'll have the bloody door off the hinges if I don't!"
Mum let him in.
"Come on, upstairs where we can talk, Arthur"
They were upstairs for ages. We entertained ourselves in the back room, whilst Auntie Shirley seemed to be very busy: moving cushions, getting us drinks, moving ornaments, then repeatedly opening the door and listening at the foot of the stairs.
It was probably an hour or so before the two of them emerged from upstairs. I remember having a feeling of excited anticipation that she was going to leave him for good. but was devastated when we were all put back into the car and taken home.

FAMILY LIFE?
Life in the Cooper household was never easy. My stepdad made it quite clear that he hated me. Surprisingly, far from coming to my aid, my mother adopted the approach that she too would join in my persecution. Every opportunity that they had to torment me, they did so. Both of them went out of their way to make my life a complete misery and if I complained, I was punched and kicked by my stepfather, and he regularly beat me with his leather belt.

We had two Alsation dogs which were kept in the yard at the back of the house but the animals were far from family pets. Every day either myself or Vicky had to clean up all the mess that the dogs had made. It was a disgusting job and one which I loathed so, more often than not I would be ordered to do it. When I was inside the pen, my stepdad would delight in banging a piece of wood on the fence to annoy the dogs, which would bark, bare their teeth and then nip at me. I was terrified that they would attack me, but this was one of Arthur's little games and he kept a piece of wood handy in the yard, to bang on the fence with. I lived from day to day wondering if this would be the day that the dogs ripped out my throat.

Sometime after Kelly was born, I made the mistake of bringing down on myself the almighty wrath of my mother and stepdad. Both of them were smokers and they always left matches and cigarettes around the house. Most days they would be sleeping off hangovers, my mother only getting up reluctantly to tend to the needs of the baby.
I think that at this point in time Arthur was away working in Saudi Arabia and me and Vicky were often left to fend for ourselves. I was probably about seven years old on the day that I very stupidly took a box of matches and started playing with them on the stairs. I had an old comic, and I was lighting the corners of a page then blowing out the flame, and then I was trying to rekindle the fire by blowing on the glowing embers. It never entered my head that it would get out of hand, but suddenly the whole page was alight. I started to wave the comic around but then more pages caught on fire. I knew that I was in trouble. I was at the top of stairs, frantically trying to think of what to do. Then….I had it…the window! I would throw the whole burning mess out into the garden. The nearest door was to the bedroom with the cot in it where Kelly was sleeping peacefully. By now the comic was well alight and before I could reach the window the flames had reached my fingers, so I threw the comic to the floor and started stamping on it.

Well, of course all of the commotion had woken up my mum and she rushed out of the bedroom to see what was going on. When she saw all of the smoke and the comic ablaze on the floor next to Kelly's cot, she went hysterical.
"You jealous little bastard!".
She smacked me around the head. I think that I probably did deserve that smack, but for nearly setting the house on fire, not for trying to kill my baby sister. She screamed at me, over and over again, that I was jealous. She punched and smacked me and said that she was going to send me away. I wasn't jealous of Kelly. I loved her. She was my baby sister and weren't the three of us going to be the very best of friends for ever? Wasn't I going to be the big brother who looked after her, who she could look up to? That feeling of injustice has stayed with me into my adult life. Nothing that I could say would change her mind. My mother had decided that apart from being the worthless piece of shit that she knew I was, I was also capable of murder. She wanted me out of the house and out of her life.

SOCIAL SERVICES

Very soon after the fire incident and as far as I was concerned, very unexpectedly, a woman arrived from social services. Her name was Roisin Rafferty (pronounced Rosheen) and she was Irish….and she had come to take me into care. I begged and cried to my mother not to make me go with her, because even though I was unhappy at home, I loved my sisters, and I did not want to be parted from them. Vicky cried and begged mum not to send me away, but the woman took me by the arm, and I was taken out to her car. I felt hollow, yet despair and fear were filling every inch of my body. I cried for the entirety of the journey. I was frightened. I was seven years old. As we arrived at Beechmount Children's Home in Altrincham, I remember feeling so small as we drove up the tree-lined drive. Looking out of the car window, the trees stood like sentries guarding the prison ahead. The huge building was forbidding and, as we approached, I was shaking from head to toe. We were met at the front door by Mr. Wall, an appropriately named massive man with a beard. He towered over me as I stood in the shadow of Mrs. Rafferty. Was he to be my gaoler?

On the left, there was a big lounge with about sixteen to twenty children inside. A few adults intermingled amongst them, and two further members of staff stood in the doorway. I was told to go in and sit down which I did, finding an empty seat and trying not to look at any of the other children. My paperwork was processed, and I was admitted as a voluntary care case, which I understand meant that although my mother had given me into the care of the local authorities, she could remove me at her discretion.

By this time, I was badly in need of the toilet, so I stood up and asked for directions. One of the staff shouted and told me to sit down and raise my hand. I put my hand up and was escorted to the toilet by a female staff member. She waited outside, then brought me back to the room where I was told to sit once more. Where on earth was I? What sort of place was this that my mother had sent me to? All of the children were sitting in silence. Some were watching television, but no-one was allowed to speak unless they put their hand up. What kind of punishment was this to be? What would my sister Vicky be doing now? Was mum going to come for me soon and say that she had just wanted to teach me a lesson?

That afternoon we were told to line up, in single file, to go into the hall for tea. As I reached the door, one of the staff members pulled me to one side and told me to go into a small adjoining room and wait there. The room was empty and smelled of paint. The edge of the carpet was fraying along one wall where it had been badly fitted. I sat and waited, and stared, and waited. I fidgeted on the chair and sat on my hands. I counted the lengths of my breaths in and my breaths out. It was silent but I could hear my own thoughts.
What was happening now? Wasn't I going to be allowed to eat?
A smell of gravy had been lingering around the corridors since three o'clock and even though I still had a sick, empty feeling in the pit of my stomach, I could feel it churning with hunger pangs.
Surely, they could hear my stomach rumbling. The door was opening.

Uncle Arthur and Auntie Dot stood in the doorway with a member of staff. I felt my throat tighten and I swallowed hard.
In they came. Three serious faces. I stood up but I couldn't speak. Uncle Arthur had his arms around me, holding me tight. Was that me crying? Auntie Dot had tears in her eyes. Uncle Arthur was talking.
"No relative of mine is staying in a kids' home, come on, get your stuff, you're coming home, and you're going to come and live with us"

AUNTIE DOT AND UNCLE ARTHUR

Auntie Dot and Uncle Arthur had a house in Flixton in Manchester. They already had three children of their own: Stephen was a few years younger than me and then there were two daughters, Gemma and Nicky.

Dot and Arthur took me upstairs to show me my room and I remember looking out into the back garden. There was a bed and chest of drawers in the room, and they'd put some of Stephen's toys in there for me. This was what it was like to be a child? I was amazed. In the kitchen, Dot poured me a glass of orange juice and Uncle Arthur got out some board games which he played with me and Stephen. The home environment that I was used to was filled with anger, drinking, shouting, arguing and fighting. This was a real home, and I was welcomed into the family. For the first time, I knew that there was more to life than the one that I had been living

The next day, Auntie Dot asked me if I wanted to help her to do some cooking, to mix some dough and make some cakes. We'd never even seen or eaten cakes at home, never mind made them ourselves. It was probably such a small thing to Dot but to me, it gave me hope and with the cakes came a taste of happiness.

For the first time, I had routine in my life. I also had the free run of the house, but bedtimes were set and adhered to and now I had pyjamas which was a novelty. I started at a new school and things were going well. I could come home from school without the worry of being beaten up as soon as I got in the door. For once life was good.

One day, Uncle Arthur asked me if I could have anything that I wanted, what would it be. To this day, I don't know why my answer was "chickens" but at the time, it was obviously something that I had considered! That afternoon, we all went down to the local farm, and we bought six chickens. When we got back, Uncle Arthur, Stephen and I set about building a pen in the back garden. That finished, we then emptied out the shed and built six little cubicles and filled them with hay: My own chicken farm! .. bearing in mind that this was a semi-detached house in the suburbs of Manchester! The best thing was that they belonged to me. They were mine, all six of them. I owned something. What a feeling! For the first week, every morning before school and every afternoon and evening, I would race to the shed and check for eggs. None! I found out that a move can upset the laying rhythm for a week or so. I had to be patient. Almost two weeks later, I came home from school to find Dot in the kitchen peeling potatoes, and she asked me to check on the chickens. Years later she told me that she had seen that they had laid but she wanted me to be the first to find the eggs.

The shed felt warm as I went in. In the second box that I checked I couldn't believe it…there was my first egg. For a moment I was Charlie, and this was my golden ticket. I ran back to the house to show Dot.
"Have they laid any eggs?" she dropped the peeler into the bowl of water and grabbed the tea-towel.
"Yes! Look!" I held out my hand to show her my prize.
"Do you want to eat your first egg?"
I said that I did, so Dot cracked the egg into a frying pan, and she made me the most beautiful fried egg sandwich that I've ever had in my life. From then on, we collected eggs every day.

I got on really well living with my cousins and Auntie and Uncle and they are some of the happiest memories that I have of my childhood. I was a different child when I lived with them, well for once I could be a child. I did let myself down badly though on one occasion and it taught me to consider the consequences of my actions. If ever there was a lesson stripped to its bones this must be it.
The precursor to events: I went with Stephen to play with a couple of his friends at a neighbours'. We were playing with a football in the empty garage at the side of the house. The other three all went indoors to get a drink leaving me alone.
The cause: I was desperate to go to the toilet. I was waiting for the others to come back, then I decided that I couldn't go into their house and leave a bad smell. Suddenly it dawned on me that I would not be able to make it back to Dot and Arthur's.
The Event: I pulled my pants down and well, there… now I'd defecated on the floor of their garage! Would anyone notice?
The Aftermath: Yes, they did notice!
Stephen and I were back at home with Dot and Arthur. We were all sitting at the table having tea when there was a knock at the door. It was the dad of one of the lads, wanting to know which dirty little bleeder had shit on his garage floor. I suppose that he guessed it was me, after all wasn't I the one from the kids' home, the one his own family didn't want?

The Punishment: Dot and Arthur sent me to bed. What, no belt? The real punishment was the shame and my disappointment at having let the family down.
The Lesson: Don't shit on your own doorstep and, at the same time, I also learnt that the shit always hits the fan.

Not long after that, trouble raised its ugly head once more: My stepdad and my mother wanted me back! A family war started. Auntie Dot and Uncle Arthur wanted me to stay there. My mum and stepdad argued that I was their son, and I should be back with them, but Dot and Arthur were not convinced that it was in my best interests to go, as I had told them how I had been treated. My mum and stepdad said that I was an attention seeker, that I was always making up stories and I am sure that they were very believable. Social Services got involved and turned up at Dot and Arthur's to take me back to my old life but far from things improving, this time my life was a living hell for the next three years.

A LIFE OF HELL

I have no idea why my mother and Arthur Cooper wanted me back. Maybe they wanted to punish me for being happy for a while or maybe they needed a whipping boy, someone to blame for everything that was wrong in their own sad, miserable lives. I think that it was at this point that they put a chain lock on the outside of my bedroom door. My stepdad would say that they put that chain on the door as I was always switching the gas on. I have checked; there were never any gas explosions on Kings Road. If I had played with the gas oven, switching it on and then playing with matches, as it was said I did, the house would have been blown into the middle of the Arndale Centre. Yes, I had played with matches, once, and I was punished severely. It was a stupid thing to do; I was a small child. They have never, to my knowledge, taken any responsibility for leaving the matches where I could reach them, but pushed the blame entirely onto my narrow shoulders.

I was imprisoned in my room, daily, often without food, sometimes for days at a time. Vicky was my ally, and she would help me whenever she could. I was treated like one of the dogs and my self- respect was taken from me. I had no self esteem or idea of self-worth and, like one of the dogs, I would defecate in the corner of my pen. Many times, I would shout through the gap allowed by the chain, that I needed to go to the toilet. Whenever she could, if my captors were out and there was time, Vicky would release me so that I could go to the bathroom. If I'd made a mess, she would help me to clean it up before my stepdad could see it and use it as an excuse for a beating. On one occasion, in a drunken stupor, he dragged me from my bed when he did find a pile of faeces on my bedroom floor.

"You dirty little bastard!"

He pushed my face down onto the floor, punching me about my back and head.

"Filthy little cunt. If you are going to shit on the fucking floor it can fucking stay there!"

Throwing me across the room he yelled.

"Get yer fucking pants down!"

Taking off his belt he held me by the neck over my bed and belted me with the buckle end of his belt. Screaming with pain I had to endure the full force of his drunken anger then, as quickly as he had burst into my room, he left, laughing and muttering until his rancid breath.

The next morning when I awoke the sheets were stuck to the skin of my backside where the blood had dried overnight.

I lived in fear of Arthur Cooper. He made sure of that. He was a brutal man, cruel and vindictive, who took pleasure in seeing me miserable. None of my friends were ever allowed to come to the house, but one day, unexpectedly and uninvited, someone from school knocked on the back door.
"Get that Vicky!" he ordered.
Vicky duly obeyed and came back to report that it was a boy who wanted to know if George was allowed to go and play out.
I was in the kitchen at the time, sitting at the table, and my stepdad was cleaning his air rifle. I looked at the clock on the wall. It was old and the face was faded. 4.25pm.
Tick..Tick..Tick..
The second hand jerked, ticking relentlessly past the gold lines that marked every second, every minute, of my miserable life. I did not dare to speak. Arthur looked at me.
"How much do you want to go out?"
"Very much! Please Dad can I go, please?"
I waited to see his reaction, anticipating a verbal and physical attack.
Instead, he smiled.
He was going to let me go out. It was sunny. I could take my football. My shoes, I need my shoes. I felt my heart banging against the inside of my chest.
He was opening the cupboard. Could I go? What was he getting out of the cupboard? From the top shelf….the jar of chillies. My heart sank. No…wait.. he was still smiling. Maybe I could go out.
"Can I go out please, Dad?"
"Yes, you can go out," he said as he unscrewed the lid from the jar, "but first, I want to see how much you want to go out."
"Eat three of these buggers and you can go" he took a dried chilli from the jar.
"Can't I just go out?" I asked naively.
He put the chilli in my hand and two more on the table.
As I bit into the first one, for a moment I thought that it wasn't going to be too bad. Then seconds later, my mouth was on fire. Dad was laughing. He was pushing the rest of the chilli into my mouth.
"I'll show him. I will eat them!" defiant thoughts rising in rebellion.
Coughing, crying, my tongue swelling, the blistering heat of the chillies burning the insides of my mouth and throat, I did eat them, all three. My

torture was over, and I hoped his thirst for my despair had been fulfilled. I'd won! Sobbing, I asked quietly, "can I …can I….go out now, Dad..please?"
"Tell the lad he's not allowed out" he pushed Vicky towards the door, "and you! Get up the fucking stairs and into your room, you stupid, mard bastard!"

For good measure, just in case there was a scrap of defiance left in me, he smacked me around the head.
I ran up the stairs and into the bathroom. Crying quietly so as not to give him more satisfaction, I switched on the tap over the sink and let the cold water run into my mouth. It felt like ice. With both hands on the sides of the sink, I leaned forward to the mirror. My eyes were red, my cheeks tearstained. I splashed water onto my face. I was back in control. Then the tears really came. The game was not even fair. The odds were against me. I thought of Dot and Arthur, of Stephen, Gemma and Nicky. Arthur would have put his arms around me…I could do with that right now…I went into my room and lay on my bed. I closed my eyes tightly shut, but the tears still came. Thinking of chickens and cooking with Dot, I tried to escape to a different life.

Nothing made my stepdad happier than to see me unhappy. I was always hungry and resorted to sneaking opened tins of food into my bedroom. More often than not, it would be tins of baked beans, as these were not so easily missed. I would hide my secret stash under my bed. Actually, it was in the same place as the bottle that I used to urinate in but as a child that was the least of my worries. Vicky would empty my pee bottle if I couldn't do it undetected. Before I had the idea of getting a bottle I did pee once in the bottom of my empty drawers as anything was better than doing it where the monster would discover it. I would have done it out of the window, but he had nailed it closed. My room was sparsely decorated. The wallpaper was pink but had been partly ripped off. Kelly had been in the room whilst I was at Dot and Arthur's and my mum and stepdad must have decided to decorate but then lost interest. There were no toys, just a bed and an old chest of drawers but I don't remember ever having clothes in them. I think that my mum did the washing, but I would just pull out what I needed from the dry pile. I don't remember ironing being done or clothes put away.

On one particular day and I remember it clearly, I couldn't find any underpants. I'd been through the pile twice, but I couldn't even find any dirty ones that I could put on.
"Mum, have I got any pants anywhere?"
"Look in the fucking ironing pile. Do you want me to do everything for you?"
"I have looked. I can't find any."
She stamped over to the washing, which was heaped on a chair, putting her lit cigarette on the edge of the kitchen worktop. Blowing the smoke through pursed lips, she started to rummage through the pile.
"Fucking useless, you are"
She reminded me of this every day lest I should forget.
She pulled out a pair of Vicky's knickers and threw them at me.
"Here, put them on."
"They're Vicky's" I objected, "I can't put them on"
"Don't be so fucking soft, just get 'em on, no-one is going to fucking see 'em"
I looked at the pink underwear in my hand. The leg holes were trimmed in lace and on the front, there was a picture of a teddy bear holding a balloon.
"Just fucking get 'em on and get to fucking school!"
The argument was over, and I was going to school in my sister's underwear.

2.00pm. P.E.
Oh my god! Now what was I going to do? Stay calm, just say you've forgotten your kit and can you be excused. Stay calm. No-one knows. They're all getting changed.
"Sir?"
"Yes?"
"I haven't got me kit, Sir"
He's not answering.
"Sir?...I haven't got me kit, can I be excused Sir?"
"Sit there, Cooper, the rest of you, get changed!"
I was going to get away with it. Normally those kids that had been excused from P.E. would have to sit and do lines.
He's coming back in...oh god..oh god...what's he got?
"Here Cooper, get these on." He handed me a pair of navy shorts and a polo shirt which he had taken out of the Lost Property box.
"You don't need plimsolls, we're inside today" he added helpfully.
No-where to run. No-where to hide.

"Come on lad, get changed!" he bellowed "everyone's waiting!"
The other boys were all lining up at the door of the changing room....all looking at me. Heaps of clothes covered the benches, school jumpers hung with the pegs pointing out through the material. Pointing at me. Everyone waiting. Black shoes scattered across the floor. I kicked my shoes off and tucked my socks deep inside them. On the bench opposite was a neatly folded jumper and beneath, two polished black shoes had been placed side by side. Whose were those, so meticulously organised?
"Come on lad! What are you messing about at? Get changed! NOW!"
Back to reality, I slid my trousers down whilst remaining seated on the bench, raising my bottom only slightly to slip the material underneath.
"He's got pink pants on" one of the waiting boys observed.
"HE'S GOT GIRLS' KNICKERS ON!" another boy shared with the line.
I didn't look up. I stood then and quickly pulled on the shorts accompanied by shrieks of laughter.
Jeering! Laughing!
"Don't you all know my life is a living hell, why don't you all fuck off!" I shouted inside my head. Outside I was quiet. What was the point?
The boys were howling with laughter, and one had a hand on his waist, the other arm outstretched in a limp-wristed pose.
"D'ya like teddies?!" he shouted in an effeminate tone.
"QUIET!" shouted Mr. Sweeney "single file! Now, into the gym!"
He put a supportive arm on my shoulder. As the last boy filed out, he asked,
"Why on earth didn't you say something?"
"What was I supposed to say?...that me mum has made me come to school in my sister's knickers?"
"You should have said something. I wouldn't have done that. I'm sorry. Come on, son"
With an arm around my shoulder, he guided me out of the door. The rest of the boys had gone into the gym. Opening the door, he yelled,
"You lot, sit quietly until I get back....and I mean quiet!"

He took me to the headmaster's office. I remember them being very supportive, but I can't remember any consequences of this event. I suppose a report must have been made.

TINNED RICE PUDDING AND THE DOGS' DINNER

I always dreaded getting home from school if my stepdad was home. It was a fearful existence. At best, it would be a slap around the head, but I could be punched and kicked, and he belted me at every opportunity. One day I got in from school and as soon as I closed the door, I knew that something was wrong. The house was quiet, but I knew that Vicky had just come in. Walking into the kitchen, I was greeted by my mum and stepdad, standing in silence, an open tin of rice pudding was in the middle of the table. Vicky was standing next to them. Without speaking, she looked at me and then at the rice pudding.

"Perhaps you can help, you little bastard, what the fuck's this?" mum shouted

I looked at Vicky, who was looking straight back at me, right into my eyes. A silent question, she was asking if I'd had the rice pudding.

"I haven't had it!" I said aloud.

"Well, one of you must have fucking had it" she pushed me over towards Vicky.

My stepdad was standing behind, arms folded, judgemental, enjoying the trial.

"If one of you doesn't own up, yer both going to get the belt" mum pushed us over the table.

"Give me yer belt, Arthur"

She started to whip the strap as hard as she could over our backsides.

"'ere', give it 'ere" Arthur said, forever helpful.

He began belting us both.

"It was me, it was me!"

Vicky was shouting.

She got a couple extra for good measure. Then after uttering a few more profanities, we were both sent to bed.

We slept that night and for a few nights more, both believing that the other had eaten the tin of rice pudding. That was until Kelly admitted to us that in fact it was her that had committed this heinous crime but, obviously, she was above suspicion.

Kelly knew that she was untouchable. She never got the belt, not that I would have wished her to. I would gladly have taken any punishment to save either of my sisters.

As she got older though, she seemed to enjoy getting me into trouble whenever she could. I don't blame her for that, even now, as she was following the example being set by her parents.

"I'm telling Dad!" was one of her favourite taunts.

One tea-time the three of us, she, Vicky and me, were sitting around the table in the kitchen. The previous week my stepdad had brought home a huge sack of potatoes and a big tray of eggs. Every night since then we were given fried egg and chips to eat for our tea. My egg wasn't properly cooked: most of the white had a slimy film of uncooked albumen on the top. I couldn't eat it so Vicky said that she would take it.
"I'm telling Dad!"
The alarm had been sounded.
Arthur threw the door open.
"What the fuck's going on in here?"
Kelly obliged with the truth, "George just gave his egg to Vicky"
"What yer giving yer egg to her for?"
"I just can't eat it. It was all gooey and runny. We've had egg and chips every night this week, can't we have something else?" As if that wasn't bad enough, I then heard myself say, "The dogs eat better than us".
Too late....I'd said it now. I was going to get belted.
"Oh, the fucking dogs eat better than you, do they?... Vicky, butter me a couple of bits of bread."
The dog food was stacked by the back door. He grabbed a tin and snatching the butterfly can opener from the drawer, he started winding it around the lid.
"I'll show you...the fucking dogs eat better than you, do they? Well, you can have some of what the dogs are having then!"
With that he started spreading the dog food onto the bread that Vicky had buttered. She stepped back in disgust, anticipating what was about to happen. He put the other slice on top and pressed it down with the palm of his hand. Brown jelly oozed from the sides of the sandwich.
"Right, you can fucking eat that!"

He threw the sandwich down on the table in front of me. I shouted for my mum hoping that for once she would draw the line. Instead, she stayed to watch. No amount of pleading was enough. Gagging and heaving, I had to endure mouthful by mouthful whilst he bombarded me with abuse, slapping me about the head if I dared to hesitate. Kelly and Vicky sat in silence, occasionally heaving. Choking on tears and dog food, finally it was over. He was a bully and a monster, and I hated him. I could not respect a man who could treat anyone that way.
Defiance was useless, but then so was compliance. I just had to accept that these were the cards that I had been dealt and somehow, I just had to survive.

HARSH LESSONS

Arthur made sure that I was afraid of him. He wanted me to live on a knife-edge.

He kept a couple of air rifles which he used for shooting rabbits, and cleaning of these weapons was done quite regularly; he could be meticulous about some things. Like himself, his guns were always well presented when out of the house. He would not court criticism. If only the people who took him at face value could see what went on inside those four walls.

One day, I was with him in the living room, and I think that mum was in bed, sleeping off a hangover. My stepdad was sitting on the couch, wiping over the barrel of his weapon with a cloth. I had just made him a cup of tea. That was another of my jobs: to make tea, as and when required. The wrong colour would be rewarded with a smack to the head.

"Get behind that chair and stick yer hand up."

He was loading pellets into his air rifle as he spoke.

"Why, what are you going to do?"

"Just get behind the chair and stick yer fucking hand up…do as you are told. If you don't, I'll shoot you in the fucking head. Get over there!"

That day he used me as target practice. I screamed with pain as the pellet hit
me, deflected by a bone in my hand. I clutched my hands together on my chest, squealing in pain.

"Come here, you soft bastard."

He looked at the wound.

"It's only like a fucking blister you mard twat. Now get on and do the vacuuming before yer mother gets up."

I didn't need hospital treatment, but I was left with yet another mental scar.

I wasn't an angel, by any means and I suppose looking back that I felt worthless. I had no self-esteem or self-respect. I didn't know what discipline was because my whole life was one long nightmare. I'm ashamed to say, that once I made some forged pound coins and I passed one off for 50p change with an old lady that lived up the road. Enterprisingly, I stuck two old one-pence coins together and covered them with gold foil paper from an empty packet of my mum's Benson and Hedges cigarettes. Mum was forever sending me up the road to get change for the electricity meter, so once I'd made my coins I knew

where I could change it. The lady's eyesight must have been bad! Afterwards I went to the shop and bought sweets, but when I got back home, mum was waiting, arms folded.
"What the fuck have you been up to now, you little bastard?"
Smack.

She held the foil covered coins out in the palm of her hand. I knew the game was up.
The best thing that my mother ever did for me happened next: She took me to the police station. I have pondered long and hard, in later life, as to her reasons for doing this, as outwardly it appears to be the action of a responsible, caring parent, who wants to teach her son right from wrong. I can only think that she did it as a public show to reflect what she wanted people to think were her own values. Whatever the reason, I thank her for the lesson.

At the police station, I was put into a cell for a short time, supposedly whilst my mother was being questioned. I imagine that they all sat down and had a cup of tea. Now I realise that it must have been a staged performance by the officers on duty, but they frightened me into thinking that I might go to prison. One said that I could be done for counterfeiting and theft. I was absolutely terrified and when they eventually allowed me to go home, I swore to myself that I would not get into trouble with the police. However, as you will later learn, I have had a couple of run-ins with the long arm of the law, but I still very much respect the police and the job that they do.

ST.JOSEPH'S PENNY

The school that I was attending at that time was Roman Catholic and one day we were all given collection boxes for 'St. Joseph's Penny'. They were small rectangular cardboard boxes which the class was told to take home to collect loose change from family and friends to raise money for the charity. When I arrived home, I put my box proudly in the middle of the kitchen table.

"What the fuck is that?" My stepdad picked it up and dropped it back onto the table, after reading what it said on the side.

"It's a collection box to put some money in." I said innocently.

"Well, I'm not giving you any fucking money," he said picking it up once more, "you'll have to ask the fucking neighbours."

He thrust the box into my hands. Then he sat down with his newspaper and a cup of tea.

I went upstairs to the bathroom and after urinating with a flourish three times around the pan, I put Arthur's comb through my hair, polished my shoes on the backs of my trouser legs and still in my school uniform, I set off as instructed, to visit other houses in the street.

After about an hour, I returned home because my box was full. I put it onto the kitchen table whilst I went back upstairs to use the bathroom again. When I came back down the box had gone…

"Dad! Where's my…." as I walked into the living room, I saw him sitting on the sofa with his newspaper spread on his lap. He had emptied the money from my box and was busy counting it into piles.

I knew that arguing was going to be futile, so I turned around and went up to my bedroom. I heard him shout to my mother that they could go to the 'offy', the off-licence, and they came back with beer and a couple of videos.

From then on, it became a nightly routine. He had three collecting boxes to work with as Kelly and Jackie went to the same school. He sent Jackie and me out collecting money and as the nearest houses dried up, he started to drive us further afield to places like Sale, which was five or six miles away. At weekends, he would leave us out for the whole day. It only stopped because on one occasion I got caught. I had my cousin David with me, it was a really hot day and we'd called and collected at one house and then knocked on the door of the next one. When no-one answered, we were tempted by a bottle of orange that stood with two bottles of milk on the step. We drank it, as far as I can recall, without guilt or remorse. The next day at school assembly, a letter was read out detailing the incident and asking for the culprit to report to the headmaster's office. I went there straight away after assembly and admitted to stealing the drink, but I also explained that my mother and stepdad had been sending me out with the St. Joseph's Penny box every day. I was given six of the best with a strap across my hand and my mother was called into the school. She told the headmaster that it was all a fabrication, that I was a liar and a thief and that I would be dealt with at home. She dragged me from the school by my hair. She must have been doubly annoyed, firstly for the humiliation and secondly that they had lost the revenue for their nightly beer sessions.

My stepdad didn't let it get him down though, he now knew that we were a source of income and he sent me out on any whim that could bring in cash. As November approached there was an opportunity to raise money doing 'Penny for the Guy'. I was made to stand outside the Stretford Arndale Centre all day and then all evening outside the Quadrant public house in Stretford. At other times, it would be the Chorlton shopping centre and then a different pub in the evening. I was also sent out carol singing, which was always a good earner if you needed a few pints. I remember once singing carols at someone's front door and as it opened sharply, a man told me to "fuck off!", that it was "only the second week in November".

They were bad times and far from teaching me about morality and honesty, my unprincipled family, with their unethical conduct were imprinting me with their own moronic values.

GRANDMA AND GRANDAD

The only time that I was happy during these years was when I visited my grandma and grandad or my Auntie Shirley. I got on well with my cousins: David was the same age as Vicky, and his brothers, twins Mark and Paul, were the same age as me. We used to get up to all sorts of mischief and if ever we had the chance to go over to our nanna and grandad's together, we used to run riot!

One day they were both out, leaving all of us boys in the house so we started a pillow fight in the living room, whacking each other and leaping about hysterically on the furniture. The pillows were quite old and two of them split. They were stuffed with small chunks of multi-coloured foam and as we flailed around the contents were flying all over the room. We continued whacking each other, the four of us laughing fit to burst, until the door suddenly opened, and nanna and grandad were standing there open-mouthed.
The whole room was covered with bits of foam, and we were all in big trouble. I'm surprised they ever left us alone in the house again, but they loved their grandkids very much and they would have done anything for us.

My brother, Karl, lived with them but more often than not, he would be in his bedroom if we were all there. He was older than all of us and I suppose he was too grown up for all our childish games. I never really thought of Karl as my brother, with him residing at nanna's. We were not close and maybe he resented me for still living with mum, but I would gladly have exchanged places with him. Mum used to tell everyone that my behaviour was out of control, and she made everyone believe that I was a bad child. It would have been beyond the wildest imaginations of nanna and grandad to think that I was being so badly mistreated by their daughter and her husband. If I ever mentioned any of the things that Arthur had done, mum said that I was an attention seeker and that I made up stories. Eventually I gave up trying to tell any of the family because my mum and stepdad were convincing liars.

Another time when we were left alone in the house, Karl was upstairs in his room with his new girlfriend. Me, David, Mark and Paul were playing in the living room. Nanna had left us at home whilst she went off to have a game of bingo and grandad was at the pub. We were always boisterous, no matter whether we were inside or out of the house. I can't remember who suggested it, but we started up a game of 'ticky',

frantically chasing each other, even though we were in a confined space. The consequence was that I ended up smashing through the living room door, a wooden surround with a frosted piece of plastic in the middle. Luckily, I wasn't injured but the door was in a right mess! It was irreparable: shards of plastic were strewn over the room. The twins started to panic.
"Grandad's going to kill us!"
Clasping my hands to my head I tried to think. There had to be a way out. We couldn't be in trouble again. Like a bolt from the blue, it came to me.
"Right! Wait here!" I rushed off up the stairs.
Karl's bedroom door was closed, and I could hear loud music, the bass like a rhythmic hum. Grabbing a bath towel out of the airing cupboard I raced back downstairs, jumping the last three.
"What are you going to do with that?" David asked with a scornful look on his face.

I took the towel and threw it over the top of the door, so it hung down over most of the hole. Then I got everyone into the living room, and we closed the door until it held the towel in place. One of the twins had collected up the plastic which we slid behind the sofa. Right at that moment, Mark shouted that grandad was coming. He'd seen him staggering up the path, having enjoyed his afternoon at the pub.
David, Paul and Mark sat on the sofa, and I jumped quickly to sit on the chair opposite. We heard grandad fiddling with his key in the front door… and then he was in…

My heart was pounding, the twins looked worried. David was sitting with his head in his hands. Then….in he came…. through the hole…taking the towel with him and landing in a heap on the carpet! He'd had more than a few pints at the pub, and he was disorientated and confused as to what had happened.
"What the….?"
"You've fallen through the door, grandad" I said, taking the towel from over his head and dropping it behind the sofa.
I looked at the twins and David who were in absolute hysterics. It was one of those side-splitting moments that you had to be there to enjoy at its funniest.
"You're alright! Come on, let's help you up to bed"

With that, David and I managed to manoeuvre him out of the living room and onto the stairs. David got in front of him and pulled his arms whilst I shoved from behind and finally up he went and off to bed.
“Nanna’s coming!” one of the twins shouted.
Quickly we threw all the plastic on the floor and as she came in, we were in the process of picking up all of the bits.
“What the hell’s going on here?!”
I told her that grandad had come in, drunk, and fallen through the door. We told her that he’d gone to bed, and she seemed to be convinced as she shouted Karl down to come and take us to the swimming baths. She’d won on the bingo and wanted to give her grandkids a treat. We felt bad but at the same time relieved that we hadn’t got into trouble again. At that time, the worst thing that could have happened to me was to be stopped from going to my grandparents’ house, as it was one of the few escapes from my terrible home life.

At the swimming baths, we had a great time as we all loved swimming, and Karl spent the whole hour messing around with his girlfriend, Josselyn. When it was time to get out, we were reluctant to leave the pool, but our fingers were pruney and we were all hungry.
In the changing room, we had our respective piles of clothes heaped on a bench next to the lockers. We all enjoyed the hot showers, the water running over our skinny little limbs. Karl was the last one to go in. He was the eldest and took charge, sending us all to get dressed so that he could languish in the showers for a while longer.

We had our clothes on in no time and we were playing catch with one of Karl’s socks. Like a hot potato, no-one wanted to keep it for long. I’d handed around chewing gums to the other three, stuffing two pieces into my own mouth and throwing the paper down the back of the bench. David picked up Karl’s underpants and held them over his own torso.
“Ooooooo” he said, lips pursed, causing his younger brothers to laugh.
Mark snatched them.
“Have they got skidmarks in ‘em?”
“Uugh! Disgusting!” Paul was still laughing.
“’Ere, give ‘em ‘ere.” I grabbed them from Mark’s grasp.
“Give us your chewing gum.” I held my hand out to receive the gum.
I stuck a wad of gum in the back of Karl’s pants and placed them back onto his pile of clothes. Seconds later, he came out of the shower, towel around shoulder, rubbing at his wet hair.
“You lot fucking ready?!”

He grabbed his underpants and slid into them quickly, then continued to get dressed, oblivious to our smirks and sniggers.
When we got home, Karl had chewing gum stuck to his skin and the hairs of his backside. We all thought it was hysterical except him. I don't remember swimming with my brother again.

There was another funny incident that sticks in my mind from my childhood, but I can't remember the exact timescale of when it occurred. Karl had already started his relationship with Rosslyn and, whilst vacuuming in his bedroom, nanna had found a vibrator. It was on the floor and must have rolled out of sight beneath the bed where the nozzle of the cleaner had teased it out of its hiding place. Nanna had not got a clue what it was and when Karl and Rosslyn came in, much to their embarrassment, she asked them. Karl, thinking quickly, had responded that it was a massager for his muscles and said that he used it after his karate practice, as every week he went to a local karate club to train.

A week or so later, Auntie Shirley had popped in to see her mother. I was over visiting too and me and Nanna were sitting in the living room, watching something on the television. Shirley had started talking to nanna, who was fiddling with something down the back of her jumper and when she asked her what it was, nanna produced the aforementioned, humming vibrator. Shirley fell about laughing when her mother explained that it was Karl's muscle relaxer and that it was doing a great job. Nanna was horrified when Auntie Shirley told her, in no uncertain terms, what the usual use for it was!

WES AND DEE

Some memories of my childhood are quite blurred. That was one of reasons that I started writing everything down in later life. I needed to put some sort of order into my confusion. I struggled to remember why I was sent to some places, and I couldn't remember how long I had been there.

In my thirties, I visited a couple, Wes and Dee, with whom I had spent almost two years of my life, I think from about the age of nine-and-a-half. I had been in care again prior to this and these were my foster parents. From my early years, these are my happiest memories. I got on well at school although Wes reminded me that I did get into some fights! I loved Wes and Dee and they were more of a mum and dad to me than my real mother and stepfather ever were.

I loved football which was a passion shared by Wes and it brought us together. I became Captain of the school football team and played in the Stanford Lads under 12s. Dee was kind and she was everything that I wanted in a mum. When they announced that they were buying a new house, I went with them and they let me think, whether actually true or not, that the choice of where we lived was mine. We moved in and I really felt like at last I had found a family that loved me… and a home.

I never understood quite how I ended up leaving them and it was good as an adult to have it explained to me. Dee said that my brother Karl had wanted to visit, and social services must have arranged it. She said that they had been very careful to make sure that their phone number was ex-directory and that no-one in my family had the means of getting hold of it. After his visit, Karl started phoning the house regularly. Dee said that he must have taken the number off the phone in the hall, before he left. She said that he kept telling me that I should be home with my real family and that eventually he convinced me that I should ask to go home. I remember when social services came to pick me up, that I didn't want to go. Dee was heartbroken and apparently took a long time getting over her loss as they were not allowed any contact with me again. I was her son as far as she was concerned, and she was bereaved. They had planned to adopt me, and it is the biggest regret I have ever had in my life. Apparently, Dee told social services that I should not be returned home, that she did not think that it was in my best interests. She understood that I was to be returned into care for assessment, but later found out that I was soon placed back with my 'parents'.

My hellish life resumed. I can't imagine now how I must have felt then, having gone from a loving home environment back to the nightmare on Kings Road. So…this was how I came to be with my cousin, David, playing football under the railway bridge, eating chips and climbing on the top of trains.

MY ACCIDENT

On the top of that train carriage on June 14th 1984 I did not know what was happening to me. Was I imploding or exploding? I felt every cell of my body vibrating, electrically charged, as each one swelled up, burst and disappeared into the ether, simultaneously, in an instant. For a split-second I was weightless or was I a lead weight? God clutched me in his hands, deciding my fate, as seconds stretched into minutes in my brain. Was I alive or was I dead? Like a novice skydiver hurtling to earth my stomach churned and flipped and then it was over… I was lying on the top of the train.

I looked over the side and David was staring up at me, screaming. He had his arms in the air and he was hysterical.
"JUMP!" he was shouting "JUMP, GET OFF THE TRAIN, JUMP!"
I shouted down to him, "What's the matter? What's up with ya?"
"YOU'RE ON FIRE!" he screamed back "JUMP, GET OFF THE TRAIN!"

I looked down and I was smouldering, my clothes had melted onto my skin.
David carried on screaming for me to jump. I don't know how I even got to my feet, but I jumped and landed upright with both feet on the railway line. Adrenaline truly is an amazing thing! Then I sat down, and David leapt to my side and started patting me all over and rolling me on the ground. We were both panicking and obviously in shock. David took on the strength of Goliath and carried me up the embankment and through the hole in the fence and as we emerged on the other side, we heard the wail of ambulance sirens.

An old lady, who lived in one of the flats overlooking the railway yard, had heard an explosion and when she saw us through the window, she had phoned 999. David lay me down in the car park and I remember about thirty or forty people staring down at me. All the local residents had come out to see what had happened. David was in total shock, and he started shouting to me that he was going to be in trouble, that his mum would kill him for going near the railway line. He was crying hysterically and so I told him to leave. He ran off and I imagine he didn't stop running until he was inside his own house, where he could block out, for a short while at least, the horror of what had happened.

Seconds later, the ambulances arrived at the scene. I can still recall now the ambulance-woman bending over me and I was put into the back of one of the vehicles where painkillers were administered in the form of gas. I am sure that I had injections as well and the woman asked me my name, over and over again, prompting me to respond to stupid questions, obviously to keep me conscious. At this point I still did not know what had happened to me. I was annoyed and in immense pain and obviously didn't realise that I was also being treated for shock. The woman sat on the bed opposite me and said that her name was Pam Broomhead.

I don't know how long the journey took but the sirens screamed our impending arrival, scattering traffic and carving a path to the hospital. As we raced through the thick Manchester traffic, six police bikes joined the entourage, two forging a way ahead, two at the sides and two behind. The blue lights screamed as loud as the sirens, "someone is dying in here!"
"Was it me? Was I dying?"

We flew down Chester Road and over Princess Parkway and we must have been doing about 110mph! The police bikes ensured that we had an unhindered route as they cleared access through any traffic lights ahead. Finally, we arrived at the Burns Unit at Withington Hospital in Manchester.

Whilst I was in the ambulance, I could hear them radioing to A & E our ETA and to have the crash team ready. There was so much energy amongst the ambulance crew as they too had experienced the adrenaline kick. Everyone was buzzing. As the back doors of the ambulance flew open, a sea of nursing staff and doctors swept me into the hospital. The trolley crashed forward into a room where more white coats and serious faces raced around in a whirlpool of activity. There were people all over me, one cutting off my clothes, one talking to me, one unwrapping what looked like tin foil. The medical machine swathed me in the foil wrap whilst nurses swirled around.
"You're going to be alright"
Still. I did not know what had happened to me.

A doctor introduced himself as Simon Kay. I later learned that he was one of England's top plastic surgeons and I think he may have been South African.

The next moment, I heard the door opening again and I looked down over my feet to see my mother standing in the doorway. She was scruffy, in jeans and a t-shirt. The doctor told her that I was very ill as I had 68% burns and, as they unwrapped the foil from my torso, she wet herself and vomited. Simon Kay took her out of the treatment room whilst the nurses continued to buzz around, sticking needles into me, putting drips in my arms.

My accident had happened at twenty-one minutes past seven and at some point, during the confusion of getting me into a hospital, it had been understood over the radio that I was twenty-one years old. At Withington Hospital I had been admitted to the Adult Burns Unit. There they had attempted to stabilise me before I could be transferred to a Child Unit. They worked on me for an hour and a half and then I was told that I would be taken to Booth Hall Children's Unit which was approximately 25miles away. Wrapped up like a turkey, armed with my drips and an entourage of nursing staff, I was manoeuvred into a second ambulance.

A full police escort smoothed the way from Withington to Booth Hall in Blakely, north Manchester. Once again, the sirens heralded our arrival ensuring that anyone within earshot was aware that a major accident had occurred. I remember the police waving to the nursing staff, who in turn returned knowing nods and waves, a mutual acknowledgement that they had done all within their power to get me there quickly and without hindrance.

I was wheeled into the No.2 intensive care room of Booth Hall which is a specialised Burns Unit. There I was introduced to Doctor LiTung who is Czechoslovakian, and Dr. Chow who is Chinese. The room had a temperature of 105 degrees and the medical staff in there were running around like what appeared to be headless chickens. Obviously, they weren't as they were doing everything within their power to save my life. If I'd lost my body heat, I would have died of shock which accounted for the excessive room temperature. The whole joint of my left arm had been burned so severely that it had swelled up to about five times its normal size. They needed to operate immediately if they were to save my arm, but a general anaesthetic was not possible as I had eaten. *Was I going to lose my arm for the sake of a chip butty?*

A decision was made to operate there and then on the bed where I lay. I was still in shock and a drip had been installed but I have no idea what it was administering. I was told to look away and my arm was put up in a metal stirrup. The surgeon said that I could possibly lose my arm but if they didn't operate there was a high probability of this happening.

I saw my mother, one moment in the room and then going out and then coming back in…then..going out. It must have been terrible for her seeing me in that way and I think that if ever she had the feelings of being a mother it must have been in that moment. I watched as they made an incision that ran down the whole length of my arm to relieve the pressure. I stayed awake for two days whilst they cleaned me up, attending to the excessive burns. My clothes had to be cut off and charred pieces of skin had to be carefully and painstakingly removed.

All I wanted during this time was a cold drink! I wasn't allowed one in case I had to be taken down to theatre as, in order to have a general anaesthetic, I had to be 'nil by mouth'. The room was just so hot, it was unbearable and all that I could focus on was my thirst. I think that the first operation that I had lasted fourteen hours, and the surgeons were exhausted. At one point, I saw a vision of loveliness: a nurse entering the room bearing a glass of orange juice on a tray. It was like seeing the finishing line when you've just run a marathon. I couldn't believe it when the surgeon turned around and started yelling at her to take it out. The drink was actually for him, and he was supposed to have been called out of the room to have it, so that I didn't see it. My mother was told to prepare herself for the worst, that they didn't think that I would make it past the next three hours. Later I found out that the mortuary facilities had been prepared and there was a trolley waiting outside. I stayed awake for two and a half days after my accident. There was no way that I was just going to roll over and die. The shock kept me going I think and, apparently, I was telling the nurses jokes throughout the night.

Eventually sleep crept in, like a fog rolling in across the moors, and I embraced it. My brain retreated into a coma for six months and then one day I found myself walking along a dark corridor. I had climbed up a set of ladders to get there and at the end of the corridor was a white light. I walked along towards it, but before I got there, I saw a door on the left-hand side, so I opened it and went through. As the door slammed behind me, the door closed in the room that I was lying in because a nurse had come in and I opened my eyes. I was alive!

That was the first time that I could understand what had happened. On top of the train an overhead electricity pylon had arc-ed and 25,000 volts of electricity had surged through my body, causing me to combust into flames. The nurses explained everything to me and at last I got that much longed for drink of orange juice. I couldn't move as I had burned all my left leg, all up my left side, stomach, chest, the left half of my back extending over to the right, and parts of my right leg. I was bandaged from my neck down to my toes, my right arm still exposed, held the drips and drug administering needles that had been inserted beneath the skin and taped into place.

My mum was sitting next to the bed crying. I thought that she was just after the sympathy of the nurses and that she wasn't really upset. She had never given me any indication that she loved me, I knew that she was the sort of person that craved attention and I was sure that she was revelling in it. I didn't want her near me, and I didn't want her sitting at my bedside pretending to the world that she cared, that I was anything other than the worthless waste of space that she had unfortunately given birth to.

I was in an indescribable amount of pain. Think of that tiny burn that you did on the iron or on the oven, that shiny flattened piece of skin that screams through your pain barrier. Imagine that tiny burn, all over your body and multiply that pain by a million. Then imagine that it doesn't go away after a few days, that it is with you constantly, day after day, every minute, every second of every waking moment. Now you are about at the level of pain that I was in.

One day I pulled all the wires out of the machine next to me, setting off alarms and bringing the medical staff running. I had reached the point where I couldn't stand the pain any longer, I was twelve years old and death was welcome. The fight was far from over though. Having got this far there was no way that the doctors were going to let me take the easy option. The nurses came in and my arms were fastened down onto the bed with Velcro straps. My testicles had swollen to the size of tennis balls and my penis had a catheter inserted.

Every 4 or 6 hours, I can't recall exactly, I was given a number of injections in my feet. I was given regular doses of morphine to try to stave off the agony that I was enduring. I used to scream for it but, obviously, there was a regulated amount that could be administered in any time-period so most of the time I just had to suffer.

Off the main ward was Marathon House which had about 23 hospital beds but could also accommodate three parents. As I was the most seriously injured child in the unit my mother was allowed to stay there. She used to sit with me for a couple of hours in the morning then go for lunch, sit with me for a couple of hours in the afternoon, have tea, and then in the evenings she went off to the nearest pub to get drunk. She did this for seven or eight weeks and then the nurses tactfully made her aware that there were other parents that could make use of the facilities. She went home.

At the time of my accident my stepfather was in Saudi Arabia. I don't know how soon afterwards but he got a flight back and turned up at my hospital bed. I had really wanted a pair of Adidas Bamba trainers and he came into my room, put a pair onto my bedside table and said that he was going to start a compensation claim. He stayed for ten minutes and that was the only time he visited.

I was having about three or four operations a week once I was stabilised. This went on for months and months and months and all the time I was in agony. Skin was taken from my right leg, thigh and shin, and my backside, to be grafted onto the burnt areas. 68% of my body had been burned so it was a long, painful process. A revolutionary technique was tried, taking a large area of skin from my right thigh and growing it under laboratory conditions so that less skin had to be removed for grafts.

The first time that I had all of my grafts done, I caught a streptococci infection, which is a common bacteria carried in people's throats, but in burns patients it eats away at the grafted tissue. I had to be re-grafted three times because of the spread of this bacterial infection. Normally after three weeks, the area used to supply the skin is rejuvenated and the cells are regrown. Unfortunately, due to the skin having been harvested from the top of my leg so many times, eventually it did not grow back and consequently I had to have further grafts to that area. Skin was then taken from the lower part of my left leg and any other areas where possible until there was enough to graft over the large raw square on my right thigh. I looked like Freddy Kruger as it was, so I wasn't worried about the extra scar tissue that I was going to end up with. I appreciated that these people were saving my life and by then I knew that I was going to make it and my determination had set in.

It was a terrible experience seeing other children being brought in with burns, some of whom died from their injuries, and the ones who did survive… I knew the agony that they were going through. After six months, I was discharged home, but I had to return at least three times every week and was collected by ambulance at 9am. If I had any infections, then I would be at the hospital four or five times a week. I was taken to the after-care clinic where all of my dressings would be redone and where I was in the very capable and sympathetic care of Sister Anna Foreshaw, who would administer gas and morphine to control my pain. It would be half past three or four o'clock before I was returned to the house by the ambulance and this routine went on for about another three months after my discharge.

During this time my mum told me that they had applied for a mobility allowance for me and that someone was coming to the house to make an assessment with regard to this and a disability living allowance. My stepdad told me that he and my mum had said that I couldn't move out of bed, that I was completely invalided and that they needed the mobility allowance to enable them to transport me around and to provide for me at home. I was still in terrible pain, and I was in a bad way, but I could walk around. The pressure jacket that I had to wear to keep my grafts in place was uncomfortable and at times unbearable, but at least now I knew that I had a life ahead of me, that I wasn't going to die.

On the day of the visit, my stepdad sent me up to bed and he said that I had to act as if Vicky's room was mine. My room was so disgusting and although they considered it acceptable for me to live in, they didn't want anyone else seeing it. It was pretence from beginning to end and I was told that I had to make out that I couldn't walk, that my arms and legs were hurting and that I was in constant pain.

The performance was about to start: the door opened, and my mum came in with a man from the Department of Health and Social Security. He asked me how I was, and I started to cry. He asked me to get out of bed and I said that I couldn't. I wouldn't have dared defy my stepdad. I cried again as he asked me more questions and finally, he and my mother went downstairs to continue the discussion with Arthur Cooper. Some time later I heard the front door close, and I could hear voices in

the kitchen. I waited, hoping he wasn't going to come storming in. Ten minutes later my mother shouted up the stairs.
"George! Come down here!"

I hobbled downstairs, leaning on the banister rail as I went down. They were waiting in the kitchen. I could feel my heart pounding as I pushed the door open. My stepdad was standing with a plate in his hand and on it was a fried egg sandwich.
"Here!" he said reaching out to me with the plate as I went in.
"What's that?" I asked, even though I could see quite clearly that it was a fried egg sandwich.
Surely, he couldn't be giving it to me. Why? He had never made me so much as a cup of tea, ever, in my life, never mind given me a sandwich. Surely, he can't have made it? Is this another one of his sick jokes? No...he is smiling. Arthur Cooper is smiling at me.
"It's your Oscar!"

I sat at the kitchen table and took the sandwich at face value, devouring it in a few bites. I had a sick feeling in my stomach, but I didn't know why.

I didn't really think about the assessment after that until I saw my mother giving Vicky the mobility allowance book one week. Apparently, she had told my stepfather that it had been declined and she had hidden the book in the kitchen, concealing it beneath a piece of wood on one of the cupboard shelves. Each week, on the payment day she would secretly remove the book from its hiding place and send Vicky to the Post Office to get the cash. Vicky was under the threat of death if she let Arthur see her with the book and so she hid the book in her knickers. Mum would then send my sister to the shops, right under the nose of my stepdad, on the pretence of buying cigarettes. Vicky said that mum had debts to pay off, but I know that she went to bingo every week. None of it was ever put to the use for which it was intended anyway. I needed cotton sheets because of my grafts but I never got them.

It wasn't long before I had to have re-grafts done to facilitate my growth which involved being admitted to hospital for months at a time. The grafted skin does not grow with your body so further skin had to be harvested from other areas. Incisions are made, like slits, so that gaps appear which are then filled in with the grafts. I was in and out of

hospital for the next eighteen months, but during my stays away from home, no-one from the family visited. My mother would make promises that she would come but she never did. She made further promises, then let me down again. *"I'll be there, this Saturday...."*
Then Saturday came and still no visitors. Four months later there was still no sign of anyone.

I was thirteen years old and abandoned to the system. Finally, social services were called, who interviewed my mum, a statement from which interview I will write about later. It was decided that I was to go back into care.

BEECHMOUNT

I was devastated when I was told I was to go to Beechmount. My first experience of being there, short as it was, had left frightening, lingering memories. I refused to go as I didn't want to go back to that prison, masquerading as a care home for children. Representatives from social services and other children's agencies came to see me and they all said that Beechmount had changed, that there were new staff and that like or lump it that was where I was going. I said that I would run away but was told that if I did, I would be found and returned to the home.

On the day that I was to leave, a social worker arrived. I was really upset and had cried all through the previous night, wondering what was to become of me. I cried in self-pity for what I had lost and for what I had never had. I cried for Dot, but most of all I cried for Vicky who I thought I might never see again. The social worker's name was Joyce Dukelow and she was not like other social workers that I had met. She listened to what I had to say and reassured me, as Alison, one the nurses, pushed me out in my wheelchair, onto the car park. I couldn't walk very far but I was eventually manoeuvred into Joyce's waiting car and two more nurses came out to say goodbye.

The car door slammed shut… that was it, I was leaving the security of what I knew, for insecurity and a fear of the unknown and I had a lump in my throat as we drove away. They had all been so kind to me, a kindness that I had never known from my own mother. I turned to wave and two of the nurses were sobbing uncontrollably. The third gave me a reassuring smile that everything was alright, and they all stood and waved until the car disappeared out of sight. I pressed my fingers into my closed eye sockets to try to hold back the tears. I had to be a man now.

When we arrived at Beechmount Children's Home I was taken to the annexe to be checked in, where I was greeted by a ginger-haired man, with an equally ginger beard. At least the huge gaoler that I had met previously was nowhere in sight. We sat side by side and he read a list of rules out to me, explaining each point as he went through it so that there could be no excuse of misunderstanding. He explained how Beechmount was run and then, quite surprisingly, he asked me if I smoked. The funny thing was that I had started smoking when I was in hospital! Another boy regularly gave me cigarettes and I suppose it was boredom more than peer pressure that led to me taking up the habit. I had to empty my pockets out onto the desk and, as well as the usual fluff, I had two cigarette stubs which I had kept to re-light later. I waited in anticipation of a dressing down but instead he explained that there was a smoking policy in place which was called 'Five Minutes': Any child that had money and had purchased cigarettes, must take them to the office, where they would be put into individual beakers, marked with the child's name. When a child wanted to smoke, they had to go to the office and ask for 'five minutes', whereupon they would be given one cigarette from their stash. The member of staff would then give them a match and the smoker would then have to go out behind the building to an old disused toilet where they could satisfy their habit. The used match and cigarette stub had to be returned to the staff member. As an adult I have mixed feelings about this type of policy. I understand that in the interests of fire safety it was better to control the smokers than to have children hiding matches and cigarettes in their rooms. However, I think that we should have been discouraged from smoking and that non-smoking should have been rewarded in some way to encourage the kids to give up. No educational material was made available as to the hazards to our health. I feel, quite strongly, that smoking was actively encouraged by this policy.

The member of staff that I met upon my arrival was Paul Moore and my first impression was that he was a fair and pleasant character. I didn't get that right. I don't believe in stereotypes but if ever there was one perfect example for the temper associated with red hair, then he was it. One minute he could be having a laugh and the next he would fly into a vile temper, sometimes almost dragging children along to his office.

THE BOWDEN HOTEL

Despite all my reservations about Beechmount, I settled in well, resigning myself to the fact that my family had disowned me for good and that I had to make my own future. I began to realise the possibilities that lay ahead. After all, I had been saved from death's door and every day that I lived was now a bonus to me.

For two weeks after I was admitted, as was the norm, I was not permitted to go out of the children's home unsupervised. After two weeks, I was allowed twenty minutes 'time out' each day which really only enabled me to get to the local shop and back.
If a child was well behaved, time out was extended to half an hour and then an hour, then three hours. After about a year something called 'seniors' discretion' was given. This meant that we could come and go as we pleased as long as the absence was authorised by a 'senior'.

I was fourteen years old by this time and my new zest for life brought with it an entrepreneurial spirit and a determination to make something of my life. I set up a car washing business and I made an agreement with all the members of staff that I would clean their cars on a weekly basis and for this I charged them £2.50 each.
There were about twenty staff in total, so I saw it as a great business opportunity. If any of the other children were short of cash, especially the smokers who would do anything for 80p for a packet of Benson and Hedges, then I would offer a £1 to employ them to clean the cars for me.

One day, whilst walking back from town, I passed the Bowden Hotel as I always did, but this time something drew me inside. I asked if I could speak to the manager and was asked to wait in a room adjoining the reception. There I was given a cup of tea and before long a gentleman by the name of John Rafferty came in and explained that he was the Assistant Manager. I introduced myself and said that I was from the children's home across the road. Some months later, I found out that this disturbed him to some extent as many of the children in the home had committed criminal offences, such as car theft and burglary. Anyway, for whatever reason, he gave me the time of day and by the end of our interview I had won him over.

I was clean and smartly presented and I spoke confidently. He said that he would take me on face value and give me an opportunity to prove myself. From that day on, every weekday from 5pm to 7pm I would be

in the hotel kitchen handwashing the pots! If there were any weddings or functions on at the weekend, I had additional work. Every day when I went into the kitchen I would be faced with saucepans, pots and other cooking utensils, piled high. I worked diligently and responsibly and won the confidence and friendship of all the staff and management. After a month, I took the opportunity to see John Rafferty and I asked him if I could work as a Hall Porter. The busiest times in the hotel were between 4pm and 6pm. The Bowden was in close proximity to Manchester airport and many business clients arrived and departed during these hours. I said that I would work for a month without pay to get the experience. There was another Hall Porter on shift at this time and quite often I would be despatched to help in other areas, at his request, so that he could get the tips when taking suitcases to the clients' rooms. I had built up a good rapport with the hotel receptionists and so they assigned me a 'bleeper'. I was 'bleep number 12'. This way whenever a guest arrived, they could bleep me and then I could race to the reception to help with the cases. As far as the other Hall Porter was concerned, it was just coincidence that I was near to the reception at the time. I think they felt a bit sorry for me as I was still nothing more than a boy and one from a kids' home at that.
I was earning £60 or £70 every week. I would work from four in the afternoon 'til seven every evening. Then on Saturdays I would be there from 3pm till 11pm and on Sunday mornings I would arrive at 7am and finish at 3pm. By the time that I started weekends which was after my month without pay, I had agreed a wage of £2.88 an hour.

The managers at Beechmount by now had become well aware that I was working on a daily basis and objected strongly saying that because of my age I should not be allowed to work. I refused to take this lying down and requested that my social worker become involved and subsequently my lawyer, Kevin Reagan. A meeting was held in the children's home where I was given the opportunity to argue against the objections that had been raised. I said that it was much more constructive for me to be working over the road than to be playing pool and smoking at Beechmount. I was earning both money and work experience. I was eloquent and persuasive in my argument. Someone counter-attacked by saying that I should be at the kids' home for tea. I said that I had a staff meal at 5.30pm, whenever I was working, and that I could eat whatever I wanted off the a la carte menu. The food was fantastic: I had steak and chips, lamb or beef and I ate far better there than I would have done at Beechmount. Finally, the opposition crumbled, and it was agreed that I could continue working.

Every evening when I went home, I put all my tips into my beaker in the office, where my cigarettes were kept. This was to stop any of the other children stealing from me. When I got my first pay packet, I took that to the office and Mr. Lowry, the deputy manager in charge, wanted to see me. He opened my beaker, and we counted the contents to find that I had £172.

My link worker, Dawn Walker, was contacted and she was asked to take me into town to open my first bank account. After that, my wages which were about £60 or £70 a week were paid straight into the account. In addition, I was earning the same amount again in tips, so I was quite a high earner! The more I earned, the more I wanted to save and the more I saved, the more I wanted to earn. Before long I had £5,000 in my bank account and it was the talk of Beechmount. Some of the staff were annoyed and resented the fact that I had more money than them, so I lost my car cleaning contracts! I had still been employing the other children to clean the cars and was making a tidy profit. I had even recruited one of them as a manager to supervise, make sure that the cars were done on time and ensure the cleaning fees were paid.

I got on really well with all of the staff at the Bowden Hotel. Many of them took me under their wing, giving me free food and on a Friday night, when functions were on, I used to have three or four pints. I never got 'rolling drunk' but I think that 'Auntie Sylvia' on night duty at the care home knew that I had been drinking when I arrived back at half eleven at night, but she turned a blind eye as I never misbehaved.

On my sixteenth birthday, I wanted to buy a motorbike. I was told by the management at Beechmount that as I was a child in care, this was not permissible. I brought this up with my social worker and my solicitor, arguing that if it was the intention of a children's care home to provide an environment as near to a family home environment as possible, then I should be allowed to have my motorbike. If I had been at home, at the age of sixteen when I was legally entitled to ride a motorbike, I would have been able to buy one if it was less than 49 c.c. My argument held water and a few days later I bought myself a brand new Poosch Maxi. I paid approximately six or seven hundred pounds for it, and I was given my own parking space in the car park alongside the staff cars. Once parked, I gave the keys to the staff for safekeeping to ensure that none of the joyriders could take it out for a spin!

ALTRINCHAM FOOTBALL CLUB

At one of the hotel functions, I met a gentleman who was the chairman of Altrincham Football Club, Mr. Geoff Lloyd. I have always been able to strike up a conversation with anyone and now, in hindsight, I know that this is one way to forge ahead in life. What some people consider to be luck is actually not luck at all, but a way of opening doors that otherwise you would not even know were there. If I hadn't taken the time to make conversation with this man, I would never have known who he was and he would not have invited me to the Club. Fortunately for me, this appears to be a natural talent that I have and I discovered it very early in life! I had a love of football and Geoff told me that I could get involved at the Club and that he would find some work for me there that I would enjoy.

I didn't think much more of it until one day I was called into the office at the kids' home by one of the members of staff, Peter Sinclair. He said,
"You just can't help yourself, can you?"
"What do you mean, I can't help myself?" I asked…not having a clue to what he might be referring.
"Everywhere you go and everyone you meet you always make a good impression. Here, this came for you today."
He gave me a suit carrier from a shop called 'Flannels' and there was a brand-new suit, tie, shirt and shoes inside. They were a gift from Geoff Lloyd, and they came with a note telling me to be at the commercial office at Altrincham Football Club at midday on Saturday.

Smartly dressed in my first suit, I arrived promptly at twelve at the Commercial Office. Geoff was waiting there for me, and I was told that I had a job! Without hesitation, I accepted, and my life moved into its next stage.

I approached every task given to me with enthusiasm and learned as much as I could from everything that I did. I sorted out tickets and basically did anything that needed to be done. I got on really well with the Secretary, Dave Baldwin, who I had met briefly on a few earlier occasions as his girlfriend was one of the receptionists at the Bowden Hotel. He took me under his wing, and I looked on him as my mentor. Before long I was the Assistant Secretary at Altrincham Football Club.

I was in fact a very good footballer at this time and soon I was spotted and given a position playing for the Reserves as well as doing my job in the Commercial Office.
I played for Altrincham for nine months, and I used to travel on the first team bus and go to away matches. I even played in the first team in three friendlies. My life really had changed and now I was spending more and more time away from Beechmount.

REDBROOK ROAD

A case conference was called. I still had to remain in care until I was eighteen, but it was agreed that as I already had so much independence it was in my interest to move me to a place called Redbrook Road. This was an independent unit consisting of two semi-detached houses with four bedrooms in each. I'd just had my seventeenth birthday, so this was to be a big move for me.

I soon settled into my new accommodation and my new life. I moved from the football club to work for a recruitment company, N.E.S., in Manchester. It was owned by Geoff Lloyd, and I started on a salary of around £12,000 a year. This sent waves of resentment through the Redbrook Road houses as I was earning the same, if not more, than the staff there and I was still only seventeen. This was 1988.

One member of staff at Redbrook Road had no qualms about letting me know that he did not like me, forgetting or preferring to ignore that I was still in the care of the local authorities. When I bought my first car and it was better than his, this only compounded the resentment that John must have felt towards me. Whenever I came in, he had a list of jobs for me to do: vacuuming, washing up, cleaning or doing the garden. He deliberately used to try to wind me up, but I tried my best to ignore him. One day, when none of his other tactics had worked, he waited until I had changed to go out to meet some friends, then as I went out of the front door, I heard a voice above me.
"George!"
As I looked up, he tipped a bucket of water over me.
He was laughing so I probably irritated him even more by laughing too, realising that he wanted me to lose my temper.
Revenge is a dish best served cold.

A couple of weeks later he was due to go to a case conference for one of the other lads in the home, Jason Hough. All the other staff wore casual clothes to meetings: jeans or whatever they had on for work that day. I knew that it was common practice for him to change into a suit and as he came out, I shouted from the upstairs window.
"Hey, John!"
When he looked up, I tipped a bucket of water over him.

He went ballistic. I used the same words that he had said to me: not to worry, that it was only a bit of water, to go and get dried off and changed, it would be fine. He was fuming.

When I got in from work a couple of days later, he must have been stewing over what had happened as he made me go to the shop to buy ingredients for dinner for everyone, then prepare and cook the food, then clean up afterwards. After that he demanded that I clean the whole kitchen. Obviously, he was looking for some sort of reaction from me, but I just got on and did it. We had a complete clash of personalities.

Some days later, I was getting into my car to go to work when John strode towards me. I locked the door and opened the window a little.
"What do you want, John?"
"I'm going to have you, son. You think you're smart, don't you?"
Through the three-inch gap, I said.
"John, can I just tell you something? You are a complete fucking arsehole, why don't you get a fucking life?"
He started screaming for me to get out, but I just drove off and I could see him in my wing mirror, waving his arms about hysterically, shouting.

When I got back from work, John had already finished his shift at three, so he was off duty. Mark Connolly who had taken over the next shift was waiting for me, and he said that I was grounded for a week and that I was on 'jankers' which meant that I had to wash up every day.
"What's that for?" I asked, as if I didn't know.
"For swearing at John Donnolly this morning"
I said that I hadn't sworn at him, that he was a liar. I said that he was making it up because he hated me. Mark was not backing down and insisted that I was to take the punishment. I said,
"You can stick yer fucking kids' home, stick yer fucking system and all this bollocks up yer fucking arse! I'm not staying in for a week, I'm not going on jankers and I'm not doing whatever the fuck you want me to do, so you can all fuck off!"
I phoned Brian Scanlon who was the head of all the children's homes at the time, and I explained to him what had happened. He said that there was not a lot that he could do, that I would have to stay there and take the punishment.

They couldn't stop me going to work so the next day, in my dinner hour, I went to view a flat that had been advertised in the paper. It was a shared room in a house, and I really liked it. I paid the deposit and I moved in!

MY FIRST FLAT

I knew that the authorities would be looking for me, so I left my job at N.E.S. A few months earlier I had been offered a job with another recruitment company, so I contacted them and set a starting date. The room that I had was in a shared house and the woman who owned it worked away quite often, so she was happy to rent out her spare bedroom. She explained that more often than not I would have the place to myself. Financially I was quite sorted at the time as I was employed, and I had about £10,000 in the bank by then.

That weekend I was doing some shopping in the Stretford Arndale Centre, and I ran into an old friend, Jason Godrich, who I knew from Beechmount. I think that he ended up in the children's home because he had stolen cars as a teenager, but I had always got on with him and we'd had some laughs in the past. As he was over eighteen, he had been ejected from 'the system' and for some reason at this point he had found himself with nowhere to live. The problem with being brought up in care is that there is no family network to fall back on and he didn't even have anyone that he could stay with whilst he sorted himself out. Without hesitation, I said that he could stay with me for a couple of days as my landlady was away at the time. We reminisced about our time in the kids home over a few cans of lager. From being institutionalised it had been a bit of a shock spending so much time on my own, so I was glad of his company.

A couple of days after this, I was lying on my bed and above me were the most horrible polystyrene ceiling tiles. I lay staring up, then suddenly, I thought that if I took them off then I could paint the ceiling and it would look much better. In hindsight, I should have spoken to my landlady first, but anyone who knows me will know that I am spontaneous if nothing else and if I get an idea, then I am onto it straight away. I started pulling the tiles off, but they had obviously been up there for some time, and they broke up as I removed them causing lots of mess. A few hours later I had gone out for something, and my landlady came back, popping her head in my room when she arrived home. The empty beer cans and the fact that she thought that I was wrecking the place, I think made her decide that I was not the sort of lodger she wanted. When I returned from the shops, she was waiting with my deposit.

I left without an argument and went to stay at a hotel for a couple of days before I found another flat. This was my own place, and I had my own front door and my own key. For the first time in my life, I felt truly independent. I'd started my new job, and everything was going really well as far as I was concerned.

The police had been alerted that I had absconded from care, but I knew that it was impossible for the staff of Beechmount to find me. After a couple of weeks, I thought long and hard about it and decided to phone Brian Scanlon from Social Services.
"George!! What's going on? Where are you?!" He was surprised that I had rung.
I said "I'm due to leave care when I'm nineteen anyway, I've only got another nine months to go…I've got myself a flat, I've got myself a job, I've got myself transport, I've got money in the bank and I'm sensible. I'm staying in my flat and I'm not moving…and if you want to come and take me back to Redrook Road, I'll just move away again and again until you can't find me. You're wasting your time trying to get me back into care now, I've had my taste of freedom and I'm taking it."
I think that he must have been dumbfounded. Then I went on,
"If you want, I'll give you the address of my flat and you can come around, you can send someone around once or twice a week, see what I'm up to, make sure that I'm fucking doing well, whatever you want"
That's exactly what we did.

We reached an agreement: I gave him the address and he came around with my social worker. When they came to visit, I made sure that the whole place was clean and tidy, and they said that they were very impressed with the flat. It was in a good state of repair and there was nothing that they could fault. I was given a telephone number to call if I should have any problems and once a week my social worker came to the flat to check on me. Gradually this was reduced to a visit once every two weeks, then eventually the visits stopped, and I was signed out of the care system at the age of eighteen.

I was all on my own, making my own start in life, no family to fall back on. That was it… me, standing on my own two feet for the very first time.

ANNA

Whilst working for N.E.S. I had become friendly with a couple of guys, one named Robert Motram and the other, Trevor Lawson. They both lived in Chorlton, so I found myself spending more and more time over there, doing most of my socialising with them. All my new friends seemed to be from the same area and one day Rob asked me if I wanted to move in to share with him and his other half, Sarah. This seemed like a great idea, and I accepted their offer. I started playing football for a team called Chorlton U.Y.P.L. I was the youngest player; the others were in their twenties. I played in the first team, and I was their best goal scorer, so I was popular with the others. We played football every Sunday and then we'd all meet up for drinks, every Sunday evening. On Tuesdays and Thursdays, we would play five-a-side and meet in the pub on those evenings too.

One Sunday evening, Trevor came to the pub with his wife, Mary, and Mary's younger sister, Helena, was with them. She was about twenty-one or twenty-two, a few years older than me, so I think there was a bit of a conspiracy to try to get us together. I was always the 'runner' for the drinks: I would go to the bar for all of the rounds whilst the older guys sat at the table. I didn't mind this at all and quite often they wouldn't let me pay for a round. On this occasion, every time I came back from the bar, they had all moved round a seat, until finally I was seated next to Helena. I was aware that they had manoeuvred us together and felt a bit awkward at first as they were all staring at me! I fiddled with the bar mat, ripping the first layer of paper off it, then dropping it in pieces into the ashtray but I have never been a shy person and it was only minutes before I struck up a conversation. Soon we were chatting and laughing, and we found that we got on really well together.

Later, she asked me if I fancied going out for a drink one night. I said immediately that it was a great idea and so we arranged to meet up the following evening.

I drove around to her flat on my motorbike and I left it there whilst we went for a drink. We got on like a house on fire and afterwards I walked her back to her flat, to collect my motorbike. I thanked her for a great night, and I left her at the front door. The following night I took her out again. We went to the pub up the road and we chatted and laughed for the whole of the evening. I walked her home and as on the previous

night, I just said goodbye to her at the door and thanked her for a great time. I didn't kiss her because I didn't want to be too pushy, plus she was the sister-in-law of one of my mates. On the third night, she invited me into her flat when we got back and we made something to eat, then sat in front of the fire and watched a video, although, not surprisingly, I can't recall what it was. By then I had my mind well and truly on other things and I finally plucked up the courage to kiss her. I looked deep into her eyes and said,
"I've been wanting to do that for ages."
She said that she thought that I wasn't interested in her after the last two evenings and that she thought that I just wanted to be friends. I stayed the night in her flat and from that day we were inseparable. It was a passionate relationship and like many people, young and in love, we jumped into bed with each other as often as we could.
I still played football all the time and went out socialising with my friends, so life couldn't have been better.

Soon after meeting Helena, I was introduced to a guy named Brian Roebuck who owned a big agency, called Roevin Technical People. He knew of the work that Rob and I were doing at N.E.S. and he was impressed with our sales and management abilities. He offered to set us up in business using his own money and he introduced us to another gentleman, Peter Hutchinson, who was based over in Buxton in Derbyshire. The savings that I'd had put away had been whittled down a lot by now, but this new business venture looked to have a promising future and I was happy and optimistic. We were offered good salaries and a good share of the business, so we accepted the deal and set up our own recruitment agency in Buxton. The office was in the town centre, but we got accommodation in a farmhouse on the outskirts, where we could stay during the week. Then on Fridays we would head home for the weekend, Rob back to Sarah and I stayed with Helena. Everything was going well, and I thought that things were really on the up, but little did I know that soon I would be on a slippery slope to nowhere.

One day, out of the blue, the phone rang in the office. It was Trevor.
"Congratulations, mate!"
"What d'ya mean, congratulations?" I asked. "What for?"
"You're going to be a dad!"
The sentence hit me as hard as if he'd come into the office and punched me.
"Fucking hell!" was the only response that I could manage.

That was the last thing that we needed right then. I was worried that I didn't have money saved and it was a big responsibility. I thought about my future and how it would change. I was eighteen and now, before the year was out, I was going to be a father. I sat in the office for a long time, in silence, thinking long and hard. I knew that there was no decision to be made though; I loved Helena and if she was having our baby then I would be there to support her.

For the first six months, everything went really well. Helena and I were managing to save money and we bought a cot, a playpen and all the usual baby stuff. The business was great too. Then one Friday, as I was getting ready to go home, I got a phone call to say that Helena had been taken into hospital. We rushed back to Manchester not knowing what had happened and I went straight to Withington Hospital where she had been taken. I was met with worried faces in the corridor, and I was told that the baby had been born prematurely and that she wasn't doing too well. Our daughter had been born six weeks early and was fighting for life in an incubator.

She was the smallest baby that I had ever seen, and her breathing was the scariest thing to witness as her whole rib cage jerked upwards with every breath. Her fingers and toes were tiny and scaly, and her lips were pursed waiting for daddy's first kiss. She was beautiful; my beautiful darling daughter, Anna, and her life was hanging by a thread.

The doctor came to me and said that our baby needed to be transferred to the Special Care Baby Unit at Hope Hospital and we were told it was touch and go as to whether she would survive. I couldn't think clearly, I couldn't organise any of my thoughts into any semblance of order, my every thought was swathed in fog and in the midst of this turmoil, I turned to my mum. I find that surprising now, looking back, but somewhere in my limbic brain, a very small child that must have once felt loved and protected, maybe as a baby, ran back to its mother.

I went to my mum and stepdad's house, and I told them about Helena and the baby. I had heard from third parties that they were saying that I was welcome to visit, so maybe it was this that prompted me to go there. Maybe I was expecting them to say that they were sorry for the way that they had treated me; maybe I thought that they would say that everything would be alright, and we could have a reconciliation, a baby and a happy ending; I don't know what I was thinking; my brain was completely coddled!

I went to Hope Hospital where Helena and all her family were waiting for news. Baby Anna, in the incubator, was struggling but was managing to hold her own.
Helena's family were not happy to see me. They were devout Catholics and were angry that we were even having a child out of wedlock. Sitting, waiting and crying, watching their daughter suffering, their grandchild's life hanging in the balance, I suppose it was only natural that the bad feeling towards me was compounded. Now, I don't know why I let them push me out. I feel guilty for not spending more time at the hospital and I feel guilty for not being there for Helena. I should have stayed at the hospital. Helena's family rallied round, wanting what was best for their girl. They took her to stay at the family home, whilst Anna remained in the hospital. Someone told me later, that it was two o'clock in the morning when they moved the cot and all the baby's things into their house, so that the neighbours wouldn't see.

I wasn't thinking straight, I couldn't have been, or maybe I thought that everything was going to be alright or pretended to myself that it would be. For whatever reason, I went back to work and buried my head. Whenever I wasn't working, I would go to the hospital and see Anna, but Helena wouldn't speak to me.

Three weeks later, it was a Friday, and I was on the train back to Manchester, from Buxton. Rob had left a day or two earlier, as he had to take his wife and little daughter somewhere. He rang me and asked which train I was catching and what time I would be arriving in Manchester. I got off and walked up the platform. Rob was walking slowly towards me…he wasn't smiling. I said,
"Hi mate, are you alright?"
He said that he had to tell me something.
"Anna's died"
My reaction? I said that I needed some food, and we went into the Little Chef where I ordered a 'Big Breakfast'.
I just sat staring. Two minutes. Staring. Looking at the menus. Staring. Three minutes. Four minutes....is that the food? Looking at the beans...that egg, that's not how I like it.... someone is crying. Rob is holding me, and we are outside. My tiny, tiny, beautiful little Anna is

gone, and I know in that moment that Helena is gone too. I cry every tear that I have but it will never be enough.

I tried to ring Helena, but her mother wouldn't let me speak to her. The funeral was arranged for the following week, and I was allowed to travel in the car with Helena and her mother and father. On the journey, I tried to think of anything else other than the tiny coffin that was in the hearse in front. I had a weight in my chest, and I took deep breaths trying to control the lump that was in my throat. I can't even tell you anything about the service, it is all a blur. I remember being in the cemetery and that there was a small hole that had been dug earlier.
It's not right, lowering that little white coffin down there. People are supposed to be old, lived a full and happy life before they end up here.
We were all inconsolable. Helena was distraught. My mother was there, she had visited baby Anna in hospital, and she was hysterical. I threw a white rose onto my daughter's coffin. It was the saddest day of my life.

I never spoke to Helena again. I tried on numerous occasions until one day I got a solicitor's letter saying that if I didn't leave her alone, she was going to take out an injunction against me.

Anna was buried in Southern Cemetery in Manchester, across the road from the burns unit where I was first taken. My mother and stepdad apparently paid for the headstone. I visit my daughter's grave from time to time. I know that Helena must have had another child as the inscription on the stone was changed to say that Anna was a sister. I hope that Helena has found happiness and that her daughter or son is as beautiful as our little girl.

A few months later, I was in the pub after a football match, one Sunday evening, when Helena walked in with Roy, a friend of mine. It was obvious that they were seeing each other and so I left.

I moved back in with Rob and Sarah and stayed there when I was home from Buxton. I threw myself back into work and the business was going well. We ran an employment agency whereby companies would phone us up and ask for an electrician, for example. We would charge the company £9 an hour, the employee would receive £7.50 and hour. We had lots of men registered on our books and we were starting to build up a good name and reputation in the community, so we were no longer digging into the overdraft to pay wages, pending payment from invoices. Then we got a contract for a building project in London and despatched twenty men to the job. Maggie Thatcher was Prime Minister at the time and when the recession hit like a tsunami, it took the building company and consequently us, with it. There was no way to recoup the wages that we had paid out to the twenty guys for the past twenty weeks and so we jumped ship.

COMPENSATION

Fortunately for me, at the same time I was contacted to say that the compensation for my accident had been finalised with British Rail. No wonder my stepdad had been so eager to invite me over; he had already been receiving notifications in the post as his address was the contact point and he had initiated the claim as my guardian. He had claimed for his own loss of earnings as he had left his job in Saudi Arabia when I had my accident. I had overheard him talking with my mother, saying that the friend that he worked for was going to declare a huge loss in income for him and that he had been contracted for twelve months, when in fact he had wanted to leave. No wonder they had been so happy to fork out for Anna's headstone, he already knew that he was in for a big payout. He must have danced all the way back from the bank when his cheque for £30,000 went in.

I received £68,000 and at eighteen years of age it was the worst thing that could ever have happened to me. I left the lawyers' office having been told that the money would be clear in the Bank of Scotland on Monday morning. I was rich beyond my wildest dreams!

I was up with the larks on that Monday. I think that I needed to know that the money was there; it was all still a bit surreal. I approached the door of the bank with a spring in my step but still not quite believing that the money was mine. The bank was quiet, I could hear my shoes on the tiles, then I was at the counter.

"I'd like to withdraw £2,000 please"

There was whispering, checking, phone calls, looking at my identification and then…authorisation.

I was handed £2,000…in cash…it was mine and I was off to have a good time!

I walked down the road and booked into the Britannia Hotel, taking one of their suites, and I asked them to send up a couple of bottles of champagne. I invited some friends over to join me in my celebration and we got drunk and partied for a week.

After that, things almost returned to normality except that everyone knew that I had come into money. I went back to Rob and Sarah's and tried to decide what to do next. One evening, I was in the Horse and Jockey pub in Chorlton in Manchester, and I got chatting to a woman who introduced herself as Dawn Williams. We had a few drinks together and laughed a lot and before the end of night she asked me if I wanted to go out for a drink that Saturday.

I hadn't been out with anyone since Helena, so it seemed like a great idea. I met her as arranged and she took me to a venue in Manchester called the 'Band on the Wall'.
We watched a few bands there and had a good night together, then when it was time to leave, I said that I would get us a taxi, to drop me off, then take her on to her house.
In no uncertain terms, she made it obvious that she had other plans and said that we were both going back to her place, whereupon I was happily seduced.

I have a vivid memory of the first thing that I saw when I went into Dawn's house: a picture of Laurel and Hardy in the hall. When we woke up the next morning, I told her that I had arranged to play football, so she said that she would make a Sunday roast and that I was welcome to go back there after the game. After the match, as usual, I went along to the pub with all the other players. A few pints later, remembering the offer, I grabbed my bag and went back to Dawn's house. As promised, there was a fantastic, home-cooked roast dinner waiting for me, after which we cuddled up on the couch and watched a couple of DVDs. We ended up back in bed together that afternoon, then at half seven we decided to go along to the Horse and Jockey for a drink. Later it was back to her house again. Before I knew it, I had moved in!

As far as I was concerned, I didn't have to worry about work at the time, as I had loads of money in the bank. Dawn had her six-year-old son, Ryan, living with her in the house and he seemed quite happy with the new arrangement.

Not long after I moved in, Dawn announced that on Saturday, Ryan's father was coming to the house to visit him. I offered to make myself scarce as I didn't want any awkward confrontations, but Dawn insisted that it wasn't a problem. It was a hot summer's day, and I was wearing my shorts, sitting with my feet up on the coffee table. Ryan was outside playing in the garden and Dawn was cooking in the kitchen.
Suddenly the living room door opened and a somewhat gawky-looking, bespectacled head popped into view and said,
"Alright mate? Is Dawn in?"

It was Kevin Kennedy, the actor who was playing Curly Watts in Coronation Street, and I was a bit taken aback that Dawn had not mentioned that he was Ryan's dad.
Later I realised that the picture of Laurel and Hardy on the hall wall, was in fact him and Alf Roberts in costume. Kevin took Ryan out for the day, and everything seemed to be very civil between him and Dawn.

A couple of days later, Dawn and I woke up to find a hoard of photographers and reporters camping on the doorstep. The media ran stories saying that Curly's wife had found herself a toyboy. She was thirty-five and I was still eighteen, but it was only a problem for other people as we were getting on exceptionally well. Every time that I left the house, reporters followed me and the papers made a story where there wasn't really one worth telling. They advertised the split of Curly from his wife as though I had been the cause, whereas in reality, they were still on amiable terms. Dawn by this time was getting annoyed by what she was reading.

One morning, I was followed into the local newsagents by someone from the Sunday Mirror newspaper. He suggested that I ask Dawn to agree to an interview with them, to tell her side of the story and that once published the press interest would die down. When I got back to the house, I put the idea to Dawn and gave her the reporter's number. Within hours we had arranged for someone to come to the house, thinking that once we'd given them a story we could get back to normality. The interview was taped: we said that we had started our relationship after the marriage was over and that it had been an amiable split between Kevin and Dawn. Once the tapes were off, we continued chatting for some time, very naively not realising that we were fair game in the hunt for newspaper sales.

Sunday morning, the letterbox banged. The Sunday Mirror lay on the doormat. The headline read…'MY HELL WITH STREET'S CURLY'. We were well and truly stitched up! Quotes were given out of context; things were twisted out of proportion. They had their headline alright, and they didn't care that they could have sacrificed Dawn's good relationship with her ex in doing it. Fortunately, Kevin was intelligent enough to realise what had happened and that today's news would be tomorrow's chip papers.

Kevin would come around to the house whenever he wanted to, which wasn't a problem, as we all got on well together. Sometimes he would bring his guitar and we would crack open a few cans in the living room. At other times, we would all go to the local pub for drinks. Kevin and Dawn decided to finalise the split between them by getting a divorce and so it seemed like a good move for me to invest some of my compensation in a property. Dawn and I were getting on well, so I decided to make a commitment to her by buying the house. It was in East Mead in Chorltonville and at the time it was valued at £88,000. I put £20,000 down and got a mortgage for the remainder. Kevin and Dawn were both happy because they had their money out of the property, and I was happy to have made an investment. Dawn reinvested her cash in another property in the same area, in Dovecote Mews, and we moved, together with Ryan, into her new house. I rented out the old place to some of Dawn's old college friends.

Shortly after that Dawn became pregnant. Kevin was not happy about it. The apple cart was well and truly upset. He had an arrangement with her to pay £1,000 in maintenance every month to support Ryan and he threatened that if she had my baby, he would withdraw his financial support. The next couple of days I was away, I think for a cricket tournament, and when I returned Dawn had been for an abortion in Leeds. I don't think that I have been so angry in my life and when she told me that it was what Kevin had said that convinced her to go through with it, I went straight out to find him. He was in the local pub, and it was only through the intervention of other customers that I didn't give him a good beating. Someone in the pub rang one of the newspapers and the next day there was a story in the paper under the heading, 'Curly's Wife Has Abortion' or something similar.

From then on things went downhill. I was still really angry with Kevin, and I even waited outside the television studios a couple of times. The Coronation Street press office got involved and a story appeared in the Mirror saying that Curly had a stalker, with an accompanying photograph of yours truly. It said in the article that the police were looking for me but when I contacted them no-one knew what I was talking about.

From there on in, I decided to keep my distance, but my troubles were far from over. Dawn went into spending overdrive. Money was pouring out of my bank account like a running tap: holidays; clothes; whatever she wanted. I loved her and I didn't deny her anything until one day when I went to the bank to get £500 out, they told me that I had insufficient funds and that I only had £213 left in my account.

The tenants in my house, Dawn's friends, stopped paying me rent, they changed all the locks and claimed squatters' rights. I went to the Citizens' Advice Bureau who told me that I would have to go through the courts to evict them from my property but in the meantime my mortgage was now in arrears. I got a job on a good salary, but I could not pay for us living at Dawn's, my mortgage and keep up with Dawn's spending. First to go was my house which got repossessed and I lost the £20,000 that I had invested in it and now that I had no money, I no longer held any attraction for Dawn.

I went away on a cricket weekend to the Isle of Wight. It was a bank holiday weekend and initially we were supposed to return on Monday. The plans, however, were changed as someone in the team had arranged a friendly match against a team in Chorlton on the bank holiday Monday. So, we booked our places on the Sunday night ferry, travelling back up to Manchester early on the Monday morning. We arrived back in the early hours and the landlord of the pub, who was in our cricket team, opened up and his wife made breakfast for us all. As my cricket stuff was dirty, I decided to nip home and get some clean gear before we went onto play our match.

Slipping my key into the door, I tried to be as quiet as possible so as not to wake Dawn and Ryan. I dropped my bag just inside the front door and headed upstairs. When I opened the bedroom door, I saw that a friend of mine, Adam, was in bed with Dawn and they were both asleep. Dawn stirred, looking over to the door. She must have been horrified. Shocked, the only thing that I could think to say was,
"Oh, sorry, I didn't mean to disturb you."
I got my cricket stuff out of the drawer and then I left slamming the door behind me and went to play cricket. After the game, when we all went back to the pub, I drank until I was virtually incoherent. I don't remember going back there but, apparently, I stayed over at a friend's house.

The next morning, I went back home, and Dawn and I had the most almighty argument. I think I even spat in her face! It culminated with her throwing all my things out of the door and telling me to "Fuck off!" She had no further use for me.

GETTING MARRIED – A SHORT CHAPTER

I went to stay with a couple of friends of mine. Elaine Kenny lived with her boyfriend, Charlie, and they said that I could rent their basement for a few weeks until I got myself back on my feet. They didn't have a television and our evenings in together consisted of smoking cannabis and drinking beer. It transpired that Elaine and Charlie weren't actually a couple but were in fact just flatmates and Elaine soon made it quite obvious that she was attracted to me.

One morning I was in my bed in the basement, and she came down and got in beside me. I wasn't physically attracted to her, she was a lot older than me, but I felt pushed into a corner and so I just went along with her sexual advances. She said that she loved me and three days later she came in and said that we were getting married. She'd already had the bans notice put up at the registry office and her proposal to me, as far as she was concerned, was just a formality. I should have just put her straight, there and then, but instead I found myself at the Bury Registry Office, getting married to Elaine Kenny.

We both got really drunk on the night of the wedding and the next morning I remember waking up thinking, 'What the hell have I done?' I knew that I had to do something drastic. I had been drunk and stoned since the day that I moved in. Two days after the wedding, I sat Elaine down to talk to her.

"I don't know what I have done. I don't love you, I'm sorry. I don't know why we've got married. My head is just completely fucked. I'm leaving".

I walked out on her, my job, and my life as it was and as I walked up the street with one bag and £30 in my pocket, I realised that was all that I had in the world. I just walked and walked, staring at the ground, trying to get my head into some sort of order.

How did I get here? More importantly, what was I going to do now?

THE SALLY ARMY

I phoned an old friend of mine, Guy Myers. He really is a good guy and without hesitation he said that I could stay at his house. I slept there for the first night and was grateful just to have a few hours when I could be sober and quiet with a clear head.

The next morning, I got the bus into Manchester city centre and I saw a sign that said 'Salvation Army Hostel'. I got off the bus, walked back to the building and knocked on the door. A man in a uniform opened it and stepped out onto the pavement. He asked,
"Hello, do you need help?"
I did need help and I fell to my knees in front of him and started crying like a baby.
He took me inside, gave me a cup of tea and a couple of slices of toast and I sat and told him what had happened and that I didn't have any money or anywhere to stay.
He explained that I could stay there but that I had to fill in all the relevant D.H.S.S. forms to claim housing benefit.

He took me upstairs to show me the room that I would be staying in. It was painted in a pale green colour, bare except for a bed, a wardrobe, a small set of drawers and a sink. It smelled of old people and wasted dreams. I wondered what hopes and aspirations the people before me had lived with and what turn of fate in their lives had brought them to face this room. As bare and uninviting as it was, to me the room reminded me of my time in Beechmount and the familiarity was comforting. I put my bag down, sat on the bed and I remember actually feeling happy that I was there, that I didn't have to worry about the outside world. I had been institutionalised in the hospital and children's home and like the herpes virus it lives just beneath your skin.

I locked my door and went to look around the rest of the building. I had been told that there was a TV room, so I went to investigate. It contained about forty men ranging in age from around eighteen to ninety. Many of them were smoking. Any dog-ends or 'dimps' as we called them, that went into the ashtrays were hastily collected up by others, who emptied out the remaining tobacco to use in 'roll-ups'.

There was an old man, with missing teeth, collecting bits of tobacco into an old 'Gold Block' tin where he kept his packet of Rizla papers. One man, with matted beard and hair, looked like he had never washed. The weather had left a lasting signature across his reddened face and his nails were each defined by a filthy black line. There were young boys who looked liked 'smack-heads' pushing each other in a mock fight. A man in war medals had urinated where he sat, and I wondered what story he would tell if he cared to give anyone the time of day. Instead, he sat staring at the television, talking to no-one.

I stayed in the hostel for two weeks. I saw on the first couple of days of my time there, that a truck pulled up outside in the morning and two lads jumped on the back before it drove off. I found out that it was a team of gypsies that came to pick up casual workers that were paid a daily wage of £15 for labouring. The next morning, I was outside waiting when the truck arrived, and I jumped on the back with the other lads. I worked hard and got on well with the gypsy who was running the show. He agreed to pay me £40 a day and for the next week and a half I jumped aboard the tarmac express every morning. The gypsy dropped me off at the job, then returned with a lorry load of tarmac which I raked onto the area to be tarmacked, then I operated a machine to compress it. Job done.

There was one resident who had just been released from prison; he had nowhere to go and so was sent to stay at the Salvation Army Hostel. We got talking and he told me that he had a release giro from the prison but that he couldn't cash it until the following day. I lent him £30, on the understanding that the following morning he would give me £40 back. It sounds a bit strange now, but that was the agreement that we reached. He asked me if I wanted to go out for a drink, so we walked up the road to the nearest public house. We got a drink and then another man arrived to meet him and the two of them went off to the toilets, talking. He came back alone, finished his pint and said we should be getting back. As we approached the hostel, he made out as if he was going for a piss down the side of the building, but I saw him get a small bag out of his pocket and conceal it under a rock. I didn't mention it and when we went inside, he said that he was going to bed and that he wasn't feeling too well. I said that I was going to watch the television and went into the dining area. It was empty and the hatch was closed down. The hot drinks machine took 20p pieces and as I didn't have one, I put my hand up inside the machine and pulled down a plastic cup. I was surprised to see that the coffee, sugar and powdered milk were in the bottom so I pressed the button for the hot water, half expecting that it would not work, but it did…result! I took my drink and went into the television room where I watched a movie and then went off to bed.

In the morning, I was woken up by two policemen. They said that they wanted to speak to me and could I get dressed and come downstairs. I jumped into my clothes and went down to find them waiting in a small reception room.
"What the fuck's going on?" I asked as I went in. I couldn't imagine what sort of trouble I was going to find myself in now.
"We understand that you went out last night with Andrew ***** (no idea what his surname was, even now)?"
I said that I did, that we went to the pub up the road. Images of the bag I'd seen him hiding flashed through my mind.
"Can you tell us what happened?"
Now what? Was I going to be stitched up for something here?
"We went out, had a drink, came back, he went to bed, I stayed up and watched a film, went to bed, woke up with you knocking on my door."
They said that he had been found dead in his bedroom.
"We wondered if you know anything about it"
"Found dead in his bedroom? Ya fucking what? Found dead in his bedroom? What's that got to do with me, I haven't fucking killed him!"
The saying that I "shit my pants" would be quite appropriate to use here. I thought, Christ they think I've killed him.
They asked me what I had watched on the television, what it was about and how the film had ended…. Who else was in the room?
I was free to go.
Thank God for that.

I found out later from one of the long-term residents that a cleaner had found Andrew, whatever his name was, and he was dead with a syringe in his arm and a length of rubber hose tied around it. They said that he took his own life with an overdose. I don't think if he was going to kill himself, he would have hidden drugs outside but that was not for me to say. I'm convinced that it was an accidental overdose.

One thing that I am glad…and proud of, is that I have never got into drugs, well not hard drugs, anyway. I have smoked cannabis, but I have never had an interest in anything more serious or mind-altering. I had my fill of morphine and the effects of coming off it when I was in hospital after my accident. I hated the feeling that it gave me, and I have never wanted to go back to that.

The people in the hostel were all from the bottom of the toilet bowl of life and I imagined that living there was comparable to being in prison, but without the security of guards and cells to protect you from other inmates. I had made one friend, a guy named Gary Kepple. He had suffered an abusive childhood, but I think that his only crime was laziness. He was a Manchester lad, like me, but he had no family and for whatever reason he had ended up living at the hostel.

After two weeks there, I'd experienced one death too close for comfort and a bit of hard labour. I'd also had enough of communal living, I had a few hundred pounds in my pocket, I had got back my old spirit and so I packed up my worldly belongings and moved on. Oh, and I took Gary with me!

At first Gary was reluctant to leave. He too was institutionalised and said he couldn't go because he lived there. I told him that I had spoken to the salvation army staff and there were plenty of hostels just like this one and that he should just take a chance and move. We paid our outstanding bills, I thanked the man that had taken me in, we packed up our stuff and before long we were at the M6 with our thumbs out, heading south.

NOTTINGHAM

Gary and I finally ended up in Nottingham, after thumbing our way down the M6 and having spent one night sleeping under a climbing frame in a children's outdoor play area at one of the service stations. I had a couple of hundred pounds, but I thought that if we spent it on somewhere to stay it would be gone in no time, so we headed to the Nottingham Salvation Army Hostel. They had spaces, so we filled in the housing benefit forms and were shown where we would be sleeping. It was far worse than the one in Manchester if that was possible. There was a huge hall with about fifty beds in it, around thirty of which were taken, and daunting as it seemed, there were a few lads who were about the same age as us, so we decided to stay.

In the hostel, there was a notice board which had details of housing associations on it, so for the next two days I looked into getting us moved to somewhere better. I went to a couple of meetings, and we applied to one of the Associations which had private houses, one of which was called Summerfield House in Nottingham.

Someone came down to the Salvation Army Hostel to interview us and as we met the criteria for residents, we were accepted. We went to have a look at the place, and it was fantastic compared with where we had been sleeping. It was clean and welcoming; the facilities were excellent, and a chef was employed to prepare meals for the residents. The living room was comfortable and had a television and as the bedrooms were shared, me and Gary were put in together. There was a staff office on the premises which was manned twenty-four hours a day and I got on well with all the staff.

Now that I had a fresh start in a new town, away from all my old memories, I knew that time could not stand still. I had to do something if I was going to turn my life around and I knew that opportunity was not going to come looking for me, I had to go in search of it.

I sat in the living room looking through some of the magazines and newspapers that had been left on the coffee table. There was a weekly free paper, called the Nottingham Journal which caught my attention. I looked through it, noting that there were numerous adverts in it and without even knowing what their charges were, I could see that it was a good earner for them. The next morning, I rang their sales office and enquired as to how much it would cost for a full-page advert. I was told that it was £275 so I then negotiated a better price if I contracted for a full page for three months. I got the price down to £100 a page, on the condition that I paid a week in advance, which I was quite happy to do as it gave me time to sort out what I was going to put on it.

I went back to Summerfield House, and I spoke to the woman in the office. I had got quite friendly with her, and she was more than happy to help me out. They had a computer which she agreed that I could use. Now all that I needed was some appropriate software. I'd met a man in the local pub who was selling computer discs for £10. They could have been legitimate CD roms but I presumed that they must be pirate copies at the price. I didn't ask because it was what I needed, and I didn't really care at that point. I was looking for design software and he said that he could get me one called 'Pagemaker'.

The newspaper had agreed a contract with me whereby I could use my space for whatever I wanted, obviously within legal and moral parameters. I paid my first £100 and I was in business!

I divided my page into twelve boxes, three rows of four, leaving a strip of the same width at the bottom. At the top of the page, I put the header "Crossword Advertising" with my mobile telephone number. I went out, 'cold-calling', on all the local shops, double-glazing companies and any other business that I thought I may be able to sell to.

My sales pitch was that the company would get an advertisement on my page, designed by me and approved by them, basic text with company logo, and for this I would charge them £50 a week. On the bottom of the page, I explained that I was going to design a crossword puzzle, the answers to which would lie in the advertisements on my page, so that in order to complete the puzzle, readers would have to study my adverts. Genius! As an incentive for entrants, I explained that I would offer £100 prize money in cash each week and that correctly completed entries would go into a hat and then the winner drawn from those. All entries had to be sent to me at Summerfield House.

That first week I sold all my adverts, totalling £600. I paid out £100 to the crossword winner and I slipped the woman in the office £20 for the use of the computer and desk. I made £480 with just the cost of the page to deduct. I had no problem selling the boxes and it was so popular that I had them earmarked for the next three months. I was also able to give the companies positive feedback by reporting how many competition entries I had received. The third week I had 580 entries, readers that had studied the adverts and bothered to send in their forms. I was onto a winner! I had booked the page for twelve weeks but because I was now earning money, I obviously couldn't sign on and because I was no longer on benefits, I had to pay rent at Summerfield House which was £110 a week. I was losing £150 a week by going to work so I was actually only £220 a week better off. For an instant I thought of throwing it all in and going back to doing nothing, claiming dole and living rent free, but I didn't want to be a tomato all my life. I had to make adjustments: my business plan had to be modified.

I visited all my regular clients and explained that although it was great that they wanted to reserve their advertising space three months ahead, I had a demand for the boxes and if they wanted to secure them, then they would have to pay a month in advance. I then offered them a £5 discount per week to convince them that this was the way to go. I collected payment for all twelve adverts for the month and by the time I had budgeted for the adverts and the woman in the office I had £1200 profit.

The following morning, I went into the office at Summerfield House and I told them that I would be leaving. I rented a flat for £275 a month, paying a deposit and a month's rent in advance, and I bought myself a computer and a TV…oh… and I moved Gary into the flat with me.

When that month was almost up, I got a call from the newspaper. My initial three-month contract was up and they were not going to renew it. I asked why not, and they said that I was getting their advertisers and they could have been selling those adverts. I had no decision in the matter and then to top it all, the next week, my page: "Crossword Advertising", appeared as usual. They had sold the adverts themselves and taken my crossword idea. As far as I know it's still going. It wouldn't be the last time that someone screwed me in business, but I learned a lesson from it, dusted myself down and moved on.

I designed a few leaflets for local business, and flyers and menus for pubs in the area, and I managed to get together a couple of grand. Once I had that behind me, I decided to set up my own publication. I went to see a company in Boston that were newspaper printers and I set up my own community newspaper that I would publish bi-weekly, once a fortnight. I printed up a load of flyers and Gary and I walked the streets posting them through the doors of as many houses in Nottingham that we could. We asked for any sort of editorial, any stories, anything that they wanted to put in their paper and explained that we were a community newspaper, there to print what they wanted to read.

Two days later, there was an avalanche of letters when the postman delivered to the flat. People sent letters about the state of the kids play area in the park, about the parking in the town, about youths hanging around the streets at night. I received letters about all sorts of things in the community. I got to work on my computer, using the spread layout, and I compiled the letters into editorial. My first community newspaper was packed with articles and then I went around to visit all my old clients that had advertised in my Crossword page. I had laid out the newspaper and boxed and priced up all the spaces that I had left for adverts.

The newspaper got off to a great start and I was making about £800 a week. I called the newspaper 'the Castle News' after Nottingham castle. I wasn't on my way to being a millionaire yet, but I was getting a good wage, paying my bills and was enjoying life. I rented a small office and employed a couple of sales staff on a commission-only basis. After two issues, I was bringing in about £2,500 each issue and after overheads, wages, rent, phone etc, I was still making about £1200 a week.
Oh…and I had Gary there. I called him the editor, but in fact he sat at a desk and rolled cigarettes for most of the day. However, whenever I was out of the office seeing clients, he was my eyes and ears. He didn't actually work, but I gave him £100 a week and his housing benefit. That was paid to me for him living at my flat so I gave that back to him with his wages. I think Gary was probably the best off that he had ever been. I was managing to save for the first time in ages.

I put an advert in the Job Centre for an office junior and I got a call from a girl named Judy Loder. She was from New Zealand and was on a working holiday. As soon as she walked into the office, all my professionalism was out of the window. When I found out that she didn't have anywhere to stay I offered her my couch. She slept in the living room for a couple of days, but I fancied the pants off her and before long we were having a relationship. She moved into my bedroom, and it was official, I had a girlfriend.

For months, everything ticked along really well. Things couldn't have been better at work, and I'd never been as happy and contented with anyone as I was with Judy. One day I went out to buy a newspaper and I bumped into a friend that I had met some time earlier. Steve McLoughlin had been an apprentice footballer for Nottingham Forest, so on our first meeting we had plenty to talk about. He was a great lad but stupidly he didn't take his career opportunity seriously. He was forever out partying, getting drunk and who knows what else. When his apprenticeship was completed, Brian Clough, terminated his contract. Still, he was a popular guy and he had talent, so the coach at the Club, Archie Gemmel, had recommended him for a place in a team in New Zealand: the New Plymouth Rangers in Taranaki. He was going to be paid $500 a week, so at least he was getting the opportunity to stay in a profession that he loved.

After Steve left, we kept in regular contact. We seemed to have some common ground as my girlfriend was from New Zealand and she enjoyed hearing about how he was getting on. It all sounded very exciting over there and when Judy's visa ran out and she asked me to go back home with her, I jumped at the chance. England had never done me any favours and pastures new seemed like an attractive prospect.

ARRESTED

Judy had a pre-booked ticket flying on whichever Friday it was, I can't remember the exact date. I couldn't get a seat on the same flight or even on the same day, so finally I booked to go on the Tuesday before her, and she arranged for her mother to meet me. I organised a leaving party for the weekend that was a week and a couple of days before I was due to leave.

The Saturday evening arrived and a group of us went out. It was a big day for me: I was looking forward to a new start, leaving behind all my old memories, and everyone bought me drinks. I was really smashed and as people started drifting off home, I stayed with the rest of the party animals drinking until the club closed at half two in the morning. Judy had left earlier, going home with Gary who was feeling ill.

I was aware that I was drunk but I still had enough composure to weigh up the chances of making it home, staggering along the street. A taxi seemed like a good option, so I waited in the line with the rest of the late-night revellers. I was at the end of the queue but eventually my turn came, and I climbed into the back of the cab, relieved that I was almost home. I gave the driver the address which was only a short ride away. He refused to take me and said that he was not waiting in line all night to do a £2.50 fare. I said something like....

"What do you mean you are not taking me? I need a fucking taxi; you've got to take me!"

"I mean I'm not taking you, now get out!"

A huge argument ensued, me refusing to get out of the car, him refusing to take me. We were both angry and tempers were flaring. He punched me on the side of the face and told me to get out, saying that he was not taking me, that he was going to wait for a decent job and to fuck off. He shouted that he was not going to take me on a 400-yard journey when he'd been queuing up for ages. I got out and shouted back through the window, into his face,

"You fucking wanker!"

As I stepped back, he opened the door and got out then coming towards me, he took another swing at me. Don't ask me how it is possible to remember any boxing training, years later when in a drunken stupor, but I dodged to the side and as he swung through with his punch, I smacked him right under the chin with my right fist and he fell like a sack of spuds. That was it, there was no fight as such: He hit me once, tried to hit me again and I punched him once. I am not proud of what I did but I still think that I was provoked. I should have just walked away but I didn't.

As bad luck would have it, a police car came around the corner just as I hit him and other taxi drivers that had arrived in the vicinity jumped out of their cars. He was Asian, they were Asian…it was a racial assault as far as they were concerned.
Errrr…hang on…er NO! It wasn't a racial assault!
What happened had nothing the do with the ethnic origins of the driver. I couldn't have cared less where he or his parents came from, what colour he was, what religion he was…he was a fucking wanker that had refused to take me in his taxi. I was the one that was victimised…for living so fucking close to the taxi rank!

I was arrested and taken to the station where I had to spend the night in the cells. The next morning, I was taken up before the magistrate's court and given a solicitor, Julian Griffiths. Little did I expect that the legal advice that I was about to given would be the worst advice that anyone has ever given me in my life.

I wanted to plead 'not guilty', to argue that I had hit him out of self-defence, and I told my solicitor that I was leaving to live in New Zealand a week on Tuesday. He said that a 'not guilty' plea would drag things out and advised me to plead 'guilty'. As my legal advisor, I believed him when he said that when the court heard that I was emigrating with my girlfriend and that I had a football coaching job to go to, that the most probable outcome would be that I would get a big fine and that would be the end of it. He said that he couldn't see the court giving me community service when I was moving abroad. It would be over and done, sorted, before lunch….he said…

"Case adjourned!"
"What the fuck were you going on about?..fine!....case adjourned! Now what happens? I've got to come back in two weeks and my fucking flight is a week on
Tuesday." I couldn't believe it and ranted madly to my solicitor.
He said, "George, it's a common assault charge! When you go to New Zealand, are you going to stay there?"
"Well yes, hopefully, I've got nothing that I'd want to come back here for."

We then had the 'between me and you' conversation. The one that starts with, "I shouldn't really be saying this…."
He suggested that I leave for New Zealand as planned and that if ever I returned to England, if the worst came to the worst, I could answer the charge then. He said it wasn't as if it was a major crime.

The following Tuesday I was on an aeroplane headed for New Zealand. Gary? No, I didn't take him with me…He was happy, with a girlfriend and a flat. He'd spent twelve years dossing in hostels, and although he didn't get a flight to get there, Gary too had come a long way.

A NEW CHAPTER AND THE TARANAKI TIMES

My first flight took me from Manchester airport to Los Angeles. With the jet stream, all my worries blew away into oblivion. I was still only nineteen and I had my whole life ahead of me. I got the United Airlines flight from L.A. to Auckland and from there got a bus down to New Plymouth. Judy's mum was waiting when I got off the coach and I felt so welcome. I already had more family here than I did in England!

We went back to the family home which was impressive by comparison to any houses that I'd ever lived in. I met Judy's dad, Eric, who welcomed me with open arms and showed me to my room. I was exhausted and suffering from jet lag, so I collapsed onto the bed for a long-awaited sleep.

I had about NZ $10,000 and I was looking forward to starting my new life with Judy when she arrived that Friday. I met up with Jock, my friend Steve MacGlouglin, and we had a few beers and a look around New Plymouth.

I had made a great decision; life was going to be fantastic.

A few days after I arrived, I heard something on the radio saying that the local community newspaper, the Taranaki Times had gone bust with debts of about a quarter of a million or some other ridiculous figure. I found out that it was a monthly, free newspaper and my curiosity, my nose for adventure and the chance of business opportunity led me to the office. I asked the secretary who was the owner of the company and she informed me that it was a gentleman named Bruce Gilmore. I am told that I can be quite charming when I want to be and in that sort of situation I always get as much information as I can before I make my next move. The secretary was happy to tell me about his other company, Staff Hire, I think it was called. It was a secretarial recruitment agency, and they had their office upstairs. I went up there straightaway and asked to speak to Mr. Gilmore.

Bruce Gilmore was very approachable and welcomed me into his office. I explained that I was interested in the Taranaki Times and asked him what the situation was. He explained that it had gone bust with excessive debts, that he had got rid of all the staff and that it was no longer in publication.

I contacted the Liquidator that he said was handling the bankruptcy and I offered them $2,000 for the desks, computers and photocopiers that Mr. Gilmore said had been the property of the business.

Next, I contacted the former landlord of the newspaper offices and discovered that the Taranaki Times had rented a suite of offices, five adjoining rooms, in his building. I agreed to rent one office from him for $200 a week. I knew that it was no good going into the business at the point that they had left off; I had to start from scratch, the smallest room being a good first base.

Into my office, I put the minimum that I needed from the equipment that I'd bought and decided to sell the rest. I then found out that Bruce Gilmore had used a company called Typetech to design his newspaper, subcontracting most of his work out to them. The Taranaki Times had gone bust owing them loads of money, but they were receptive to my call as they probably knew the equipment that I was selling. I had about fifteen desks and computers to get rid of and a huge photocopier. Typetech thought that they had a great deal when they handed over $15,000 for the lot, but in fact I had made $13,000, the equivalent of about £5,000 in the UK, and I'd kitted out my office. I now had a bit of cash flow to get me started.

I registered the company as the Taranaki Times Publishing Ltd and then I got in touch with Stratford Press in Stratford, which was about a forty-five-minute drive away. They were the printers that Bruce Gilmore had been using. I said that I was restarting the Taranaki Times and that I wanted to use them to print the newspaper. I negotiated a price and before the morning was out, my printers were in place and waiting to do the first print run.

I had been in New Zealand for a week and at nineteen years of age, I was now the owner and editor of the Taranaki Times.

Next on the agenda, I contacted the local radio station that I'd heard on air talking about the Taranaki Times going bust and I told them that I had taken over their local community newspaper. I arranged an appointment and went in to talk to one of the news-members on the News Team. I was interviewed live on air where I explained that I had taken over the Taranaki Times, that I didn't have any journalists or reporters and that they, the listeners, the people of Taranaki, were going to make the paper. I asked them to send in stories, photographs, anything of local interest and together we would create a local community newspaper that they could all enjoy and be proud of. I said that the back page would be earmarked for sports related stories and that if anyone had a football team, or any other team, then they should send photos, fixtures, match reports to me by Wednesday at 3pm to be included in the Saturday's publication.

Copy started to arrive. If it was already on a 'Word' document, then I would just copy and paste it into my article. As well as sorting out all the editorial, I sat at my desk and sold, sold, sold…adverts…loads of adverts… to anyone that I could convince to have one. If I was doing features with sports clubs, then I would sell adverts to all the Clubs' sponsors. I had breweries and insurance companies and I tapped into the biggest names that I could find in the area who had given sponsorship somewhere. Things were going really well.

I re-employed all the paperboys and papergirls that had been delivering the old publication and the next week they were out in force in the community, wearing my labelled bibs. I set on a lad, Mark, to work at the office, to take the weight off my advertising sales. At last, I could step away from that part of the business, now the challenge had gone out of it, I was bored with chasing up adverts, so it was a relief to be able to hand this to someone else.

Everything was going well but then I had an argument with Judy. Things had not been good between us for some time, and I moved out and went to live with Jock, Steve McLoughlin, who I knew from England.

I may have to stand corrected here if anyone disagrees, but New Zealand's main sport is rugby. Jock was playing for New Plymouth Rangers, a football team, and I went down to train with them. As I pulled up on the car park, I could see the players on the field, and they were doing 'kick-ups'. It looked to me like six was the highest number that anyone could keep up and I was horrified as I could do well over a hundred. This gave me more confidence to go into the training session. I was a good player in the U.K but here I was welcomed onto the first team of the New Plymouth Rangers. I was a professional footballer!

Before long, both Jock and I were local celebrities. The club treated us well, sending a cleaner to the house, food shopping, you name it, they bent over backwards to please us and that was on top of our wages. I was still young, and it all went to my head. Jock and I were in the club bar every night and every weekend. We were always getting drunk and smoking cannabis but at the time I thought that life couldn't get any better.

I neglected the Taranaki Times, still taking money out but contributing nothing. One thing that I have learned over the years is that no-one can sell like I can. What is easy to me can be really difficult for others; I sometimes expect too much from people and am often disappointed when they don't live up to my expectations. Although I am sure that he was working hard, Mark had no support from me, the advertising sales dropped and the editorial was not up to standard, but I just ignored it and carried on partying.

WISHING WELL

Jock and I got into the habit of going into one pub regularly. It was called the Crown and Rose and we used to go there whenever we weren't playing football or out with the lads. The pub had a band on almost every night: they were called 'Wishing Well' and I thought that they were absolutely fantastic. The girl singer, Kelly, was stunning and I can still remember her gorgeous face and liquid voice. The bass guitarist was a guy called Les, Neil played drums, Kevin, I think, was another band member, plus one more who will be insulted to read that I can't even recall his name, so apologies to him. They were brilliant together, doing covers of popular songs.

Jock and I were accepted by the locals because we played in their football team and celebrity being the animal it is, people were eager to become our friends. There was a raised area at the end of the pub that held about four or five tables. I think that previously it had been used as a stage but at that time it was seating space. Every time when we went into the Crown and Rose, we had a table on the raised area with a couple of tables reserved next to us for the band and friends. Wishing Well would play about eight songs and then come off for a twenty-minute break. Each time that they had a break they were given a bottle of bourbon. This was an agreement that they had with the landlord, as part of their payment for packing the place out every night. We all had plastic glasses and Les would dish out shots of neat bourbon and we would play drinking games. Then the band would have to go back on for their next set...then come back off... more bourbon. At the end of the night, we would, more often than not, go back to someone's house to carry on the party. If there were any special events on at the pub, Les had another band, 'The Nod' who would be booked for those occasions. The lead guitarist, Doof, was a phenomenal player.

There was, and I suppose still is, a huge venue in the area: the Bowl of Brooklands. Under the influence of bourbon and swept along in a euphoric wave of success, I decided to put on a big gig. I knew that the locals would not pay to see Wishing Well and the Nod as they could see them in the pub almost every night of the week, so putting them on as supporting artistes, I contracted a well-known reggae band from Auckland, The Herbs. I agreed to pay them $5,000 for the night.

The Bowl of Brooklands was a massive arena, holding 30,000 people. It had hosted such bands before as UB40 and Crowded House. I do not know what I was thinking.... I must have been on the bourbon train to Smashville when I had the idea and that euphoric wave of success? The tide was about to turn.

I plastered posters everywhere; had advertising on the radio; my football was fantastic...I even scored seven goals in one game alone; I was a local celebrity; I was great....and I thought that I was indestructible!

I needed four and a half thousand people on the night to break-even, but I was already treading on thin ice as I had taken money from the Taranaki Times to fund the event.
On the morning of the gig, I woke up and looked out of the window. I had already started feeling nervous and twitchy about the concert and when I looked out onto a rain-soaked landscape, my worries quadrupled. Still, it was too late now, the show must go on and I still hoped that at least I might break even. It poured with rain all day and into the evening and only 1,500 people braved the weather and went to the Bowl of Brooklands. These were all advance tickets sales, no-one wanted to be out in that weather. They sat with umbrellas and enjoyed brilliant performances by all three bands and musically it was a roaring success. Financially and emotionally, with every drop of rain that fell in that day-long monsoon, my savings, my livelihood, The Taranaki Times, my friendships and finally my reputation, were washed away into the gutter.

People were after me for payment from the Taranaki Times and from the Bowl of Brooklands gig. I lost the plot completely and ran away.

ON THE RUN

I had an emergency fund, one thing that after my stint in the Salvation Army Hostel, I promised myself that I would always have. It was only $2,000 but it was enough to get me on a flight to Australia and somewhere to stay. I landed on the Gold Coast, in Brisbane, and I put everything out of my mind and had a great four days. Brisbane was fantastic. I knew that what I had done was wrong and I rang Jock who told me that my face had been on television, that I had been on radio news and in the papers, that everyone was looking for me, that I owed loads of money from the gig…and that the police were after me! A detective, Paul Carson, from Palmerston North Police in New Zealand was co-ordinating the search and I think the word used was: he was 'hunting' me!

Oh my god!

Now I was being hunted.

I was a wanted man... a criminal!!

I had to sort it out.

I rang detective Paul Carson.

"Hello, my name is George Bamby, I believe that you want to speak to me?"

An understatement I knew but at least I'd opened the communication line.

"Yes, we do. Where are you?"

"I'm in Australia."

"You need to come back to New Zealand."

"My visa has expired; I can't even come back to sort it out"

He said to tell him what flight I was coming back on, and he would arrange for immigration to stamp my passport with a three-month visa which would give me time to sort everything out.

I was obviously worried; I knew that I had the chance to run but wanted to sort out the mess that I had left behind.

"What's going to happen to me?" I asked Paul Carlton.

He said that I had left a lot of debts and that there was a question over my tax payments from the Taranaki Times.

My heart was beating so hard, I could feel the blood pumping in my ears. Thinking about Jock and Judy and her family, I thought that I owed it to them, so I bit the bullet.

"OK, I'm coming back."

I landed at Auckland airport. The immigration officers were expecting me as I had rung Paul Carlton beforehand and let him know which flight

I was on. I was taken into a side room. It was a sunny day and the window was open, but I was struggling to breathe. I couldn't smoke in there, but my nerves were frayed and I needed a nicotine boost. Even though I'd been assured that I would not be arrested, I was anxious…after all hadn't Jock said that I'd been all over the news? The immigration officer stamped my passport with a three-month visa and said that I could go on my way. I felt a certain amount of relief and I thought that things couldn't be that bad or they would have taken me into custody there and then.

I went back up to New Plymouth and I rang Paul Carlson to say that I had arrived.
He came to see me straight away and what transpired was that the police had got involved because, when I disappeared, they had been into the Taranaki Times. There I had a small book in which I kept details of cash payments that I received: items that I was not putting through the books. For small companies that advertised I gave them a cash price and didn't declare the income. There were 87 entries.
Fuck me! Now I was about to get done for tax evasion!

In Taranaki I was a social leper. I owed people money. No-one cared that I'd been running a limited company. As far as everyone was concerned, I had ripped off the community. The company did owe people money and I take full responsibility for the demise of the Taranaki Times. When I got back to New Zealand, the first thing that I did was to go and pay the kids that had been delivering the papers. I didn't mind owing money to companies, but the children were my first priority. I wasn't personally liable for any of the debts that had accrued, but as it was a small community the police were pursuing me for the tax evasion charge.

I was released on bail pending further enquiries, one of the conditions being that I remain in the country. I went to the employment office and explained that I had to remain in the country on police bail and that I did not now have a work permit. I was put onto full benefits receiving $240 a week and my share of the rent in the house with Jock was paid. I was still able to play football with the New Plymouth Rangers because I was one of their star players and they needed me in the team.

Every contact that I had with Paul Carlson he hinted that after my three-month visa was up I would not be allowed to remain in the country and

that once I had been charged and dealt with in court, that I would be deported. This was my biggest dread and the thought of having to return to England ate away at me every day. I loved New Zealand, I loved my life, and I had hoped that once I had faced the charges that I could put it all behind me and start afresh. Suddenly it dawned on me that this was not going to be possible, and that drastic action was needed. I rang Les, the bass player from Wishing Well.
"Les!"
"George?"
"I want to get married! I want to get married and stay in the country!"
Les was great and came to my rescue on a white steed carrying a Maori girl on the back. Her name was Meryl Martin and for her to marry me was going to cost $500 and a case, twelve bottles, of bourbon! Result! I was sorted, just the stag night and service to sort out now. I was on the home stretch. I think I was constantly drunk for three days before the service, maybe to numb the pain.
On the day, we arranged for a Justice of the Peace to marry us in the garden. I had quite a few Maori friends, whom I used to go fishing with. They all turned up. Wishing Well came along with all their friends. Everyone associated with New Plymouth Rangers, that I knew, turned up in the garden. All of Meryl's family and Maori friends came. There were three hundred of us there to celebrate a sham of a marriage. It was a riot; people were drinking and smoking cannabis. We didn't even have a ring! Someone very creatively cut the top off a Jack Daniels bottle and that is the ring that I put on Meryl Martin's finger. I remember at the end of the service when the Justice of the Peace said that I could kiss the bride, I looked at her and thought, "Fuck me! You're ugly"
She was a nice person, but I can't pretend that there was even a glint of physical attraction, not on my part anyway. She leaned forward and started to kiss me, and I still remember vividly that I could hear the sound of Doof, the guitarist, throwing up somewhere quite nearby. He was actually vomiting due to the excessive amount of drink that he'd had.

To give credibility to our marriage, we had arranged that Meryl would move in to live with me. Little did I expect that she thought she would be sharing my bed. One of her friends said to me that she'd spoken to Meryl who had said that she was so happy to be marrying me and that she was really going to make a go of it.
WHAT?!! Hold on a minute!

Another nightmare began to unfold.
I explained to her friend, and then to Meryl, that it was a marriage of convenience, that we were not going to be living as husband and wife, that I didn't love her, was not attracted to her and had no intention of having sex with her. I reiterated that there were not going to be any children and that I was not going to be spending the rest of my life with her. She said,
"That's not the impression I got bro'!"
I had to go through it with her all over again. Finally, I had to ask her to move out of the house. She would not accept that it was a deal for which I had paid.
I was about to pay again……this time it was going to cost me far more than $500 and a case of bourbon.

Meryl did move out, as I requested, but feeling that I had reneged on my part of the deal, she went to the police and told them that it had been a marriage of convenience.
Meanwhile the police investigation into my alleged tax evasion was over and a decision had been made to drop the charges. This was due partly to my having said that I was going to plead not guilty to every one of the charges and that they would have to take me to court for each case, at a cost to the taxpayer of thousands. The amount that I had put through undeclared was not really the issue, it was just a legality, that they could get me for putting cash through without declaring goods and services tax and it was a means of making me personally accountable for the downfall of the company. When Meryl arrived at the police station and gave a statement this provided new ammunition and an investigation was put underway.

I received a phone call inviting me to go to the office where I could be formally told that the charges against me were being dropped and to sign some paperwork. I was really pleased and couldn't get to the office quickly enough. With all the 'I's dotted and the 'T's crossed, I thought that was the end of it and thanked the officer on duty.
As I was about to leave….
"George?...Just one more thing…"
"What's that?"
"George Bamby...I'm arresting you on suspicion of bigamy"

NOOOOO! REWIND!.... Wedding...Elaine Kenny, two days... Wedding ...

Meryl Martin.....OH FUCK! I'D REALLY DONE IT THIS TIME!
Fingerprints.
Shoelaces.
Cells
OH MY GOD WHAT HAD I DONE?

I decided to plead not guilty purely because I knew that the trial would take six or seven months and at least I could delay leaving the country which I loved and had wanted to make my home.

I was released on bail but there was more trouble to come:
Whilst living with Jock I had bought a television and video combi unit for $250. I'd got it on finance, setting up a direct debit for $25 a month. After I was released on bail, we were moving house and the new place was fully furnished, including three televisions. One of my mates offered me $150 for the combi unit so I thought that I might as well sell it now. It was only a cheap telly and I thought that I would probably end up giving it away in a few months, so I took his offer and let it go. I still had a bit left to pay on it, but it didn't matter as it was going out by direct debit anyway. I don't know how it came about to even be brought to the attention of the police, but they came and arrested me for deception.
Deception?! I'd nearly paid for the television anyway and by the time I left it would have been mine. Someone had it in for me.
However, according to New Zealand law, it is illegal to sell something that is being purchased on finance. They had me bang to rights, so now I had to wait for a court date for that as well. Things were not looking good.

Whilst I was waiting to go to court for the bigamy charge, I decided that I had better earn a bit of money. I thought that scrap metal would be a good business to get instant returns with no overheads. One of my advertisers with the Taranaki Times was a company called Maui Metals. When I had visited him to discuss his adverts, there were truckloads of aluminium, tin cans, stainless steel, lead and copper. People were turning up with trucks and he was paying out cash for the metal. As usual, I had to know the ins and outs of everything, so I got talking to one of the guys in the yard and he gave me a list of all the money that could be made on the various metals: stainless steel was $1.10 per kilo, copper $2.50, lead 60c, iron $100 a ton.

One of my mates worked for a company that manufactured stainless steel products primarily for the catering trade. They made sinks, work units, air vents and anything else that you could think of that was made from stainless steel was made there.
The company had five depots scattered over the North Island. All the cut-offs from the manufacturing process were put into huge skips at the back of each plant and then once a month a truck would come down from Auckland, taking numerous trips to empty the waste skips. It is a common practice in New Zealand for the employer to supply the employees with cans of beer at the end of Fridays' shifts. The start of the weekend celebrations would then convene to the nearest pub after the cans of beer were finished.

That stainless-steel company did not condone the practice, so when I suggested that I contribute to their 'piss fund' as they called it, to the tune of $100 a month in return for a lorry load of scrap metal, the lads jumped at the chance. I would pull into the yard at about 4.30pm, the manager would be there to organise things, I'd pay my $100 and he would get the guys to load up my truck. It belonged to and was driven by another acquaintance of mine. Within ten minutes, we would have a lorry load of scrap stainless steel and, as there were so many skips at each depot, the amount moved was not even noticeable. When I pulled up, I always made sure that I had a couple of cases of beer, DB Draught, which was shared amongst the lads once they'd loaded us up. The next day I would take the metal to Maui Metals who would give me $2,300 for a lorry full, about £800. The guy who worked with me got $300 of this and we visited each of the five depots once in every month.

Before I knew it the date for my trial for bigamy had arrived. I knew that the deception charge was also being heard on the same day and I hated the thought that I might have to leave New Zealand. I knew that I stood no chance in fighting a conviction and that court costs for a trial would be heavy so at the last moment I changed my plea to guilty for both charges.

I stood stony-faced in the dock.
"Mr. Bamby! The last time that someone appeared in a court in New Zealand charged with bigamy, the man was hung."
OH FUCK!
I swallowed hard, a knot in my chest where my heart was supposed to be.

The judge continued….
" ….I don't think that on this occasion we will be going to those extremes. We are prepared to drop the charges on both counts on the condition that you leave the country."
"I don't want to leave the country." I implored hoping that by some miracle I might still be able to pull this off. I knew that my visa was up anyway, so this was my last chance.
He started writing….
looking at me…writing…
I was discharged on the bigamy charge and given a $500 fine for the deception charge. I couldn't believe it.
Was that it? Was I, after all, going to be able to stay and get myself sorted out once and for all? This time…this time…I was going to do it right…everything by the book…fresh start…thank you ..thank you….thank you….my head was pounding with the thoughts and prospects of a new beginning.

I walked out of the courtroom a relieved man…. but only for a few seconds
…not even for a whole minute….
Two policemen were waiting either side of the door as I left.
"George Bamby, I am arresting you under the Immigration Act….."
OH FOR FUCK'S SAKE…NOW WHAT WAS HAPPENING?
NOW WHAT WAS I BEING DONE FOR?

My temporary visa that the police had arranged had expired two weeks before the court date and I was arrested as an 'overstayer'. I had submitted my application for an extension but had not received confirmation either way. I explained this and was told that they were there to tell me that it had been declined. I was taken to New Plymouth police station across the road, held in the cells and without even being able to say goodbye to anyone, the following morning I was transferred to the airport and put on a plane out of New Zealand.

DEPORTED

Paul Carlson, the detective, was assigned to ensure that I made the trip, and I was handcuffed to him. I couldn't believe that I was being deported and that they would go to the extremes of handcuffing me. We had a stop-over in Hong Kong where I was put in holding cells for about five hours. On the flight from there to Heathrow I finally convinced my gaoler to release me from the handcuffs as we still had hours of flying time ahead and after all, I argued, where could I run to?

After sixteen hours aboard the flight, we landed at Heathrow.
Thank god for that, we were here and I could at last be rid of Paul Carson.
Immigration.
Now ...who are all those guys standing there? Smartly dressed...look like officials....Police?...maybe....Oh god, they are waiting for us.....
Scotland Yard
CAN THIS GET ANY WORSE? WHAT DO THEY WANT WITH ME? What am I supposed to have done now? I've been living in New Zealand for five years.
"George Bamby?"
It's definitely me...yes ...they've come for me.

Paul Carlson introduced himself and it became obvious why I had been handcuffed.
"George Bamby, we are arresting you for breach of bail."

Oh my god...all this now.. for that incident in Nottingham? That incident..."it's only a minor charge, George, if I was you......don't worry about it....."

As I was marched away in handcuffs, I was worrying about it.
The flight arrived at half seven on a Friday evening which meant that I had to be kept in the cells at Heathrow from then until the Monday morning when I would be delivered to court.

COURT AND ROCK BOTTOM

Monday morning. 5am. A Securicor van turned up to take me on the journey north to Nottingham. I arrived at the courthouse and was put into a cell where the lawyer, who had been allocated to me, came in to talk to me about the case. He looked at the charges and tried to reassure me by saying that we would have to see how it went in the court.

As I walked up to the court my footsteps were hollow and resonated throughout my body. I felt sick. My mouth was dry.

The room is big and there is a judge sitting behind the bench. Everyone is looking at me as I go in. I'm in the dock, with a glass panel between me and the rest of the world. Murderers have stood here.. murderers, child molesters, rapists...and now I am here, standing in this dock with my fate in the hand of a man dressed in a gown and a wig, a man who doesn't know me, he doesn't know anything about me. He will only know what is written on that paper before him and what he hears now. I can't breathe.
Someone is speaking.
Before we go any further......another charge....what now? What is this? Breach of bail....how do you plead?
I hear myself say "Guilty".

I was told to sit down. My legs would not have held me for much longer anyway.
The judge informed the court that I had absconded from the judicial system, that I had breached my bail conditions and that not only had I gone to the other side of the world but I had remained there for five years. He then went on to say that before I left, the case had been adjourned for two weeks pending reports before sentencing. He said that he was going to do exactly the same now: adjourn for two weeks for a pre-sentence report during which time I was to be remanded in custody.

What was that he'd just said? Remanded in custody? Was I being sent to jail? My worst nightmare was coming true. I couldn't go to jail...what with the murderers and child molesters and rapists? I shouldn't be going to jail...I shouldn't have even pleaded guilty to the assault. The police officer next to me was taking my arm. I was shouting,
"What? I'm going to prison? I'm going to prison?"

My solicitor came rushing over and the room was spinning behind him,
"What's going on?" I am hysterical.
"I'm going to prison, I'm going to prison!"

I remember the solicitor leaned over me and said,
"George, there's a lot frailer people than you that have been sent to prison before and got through it. You'll be fine, I'll come and see you downstairs in a few minutes."
I couldn't even walk from the dock. I didn't want to leave the courtroom because I knew that once I did, I was on my way to prison. The guards almost dragged me out. I felt light-headed, my feet were moving but I had no control over my body.

The next few minutes were a complete blur, walking back to the cell, but I remember when I got there that there was a chalkboard outside upon which had been scrawled two words. LINCOLN PRISON. The door to the cell was opened by the duty officer and to my horror I saw that it was already occupied.

Fear of prison and stories about being raped were already racing through my mind and my immediate impression of the man inside the cell was that he was a homosexual. Now, that seems almost laughable to me: firstly, because I assumed that he was gay from his appearance and secondly because I was frightened of him because he might be gay. He was on his way to prison too so I am sure that sex was not the first thing on his mind at the time anyway! He asked me what I was in there for, and I told him "assault", and asked him what he was in for. He'd been done for drink-driving and then subsequently been arrested for driving whilst banned and sentenced to a prison term.

Minutes later the door opened again, and a further prisoner was put in with us, then another, and another....and another. There were six of us. At lunch time, one of the officers came in with sandwiches, crisps and a drink for each of us. I was absolutely terrified but trying my hardest not to show it. Suddenly the door opened; it swung heavily on its hinges.

"First one, OUT!" yelled the guard, handcuffing the first prisoner.
One more in front of me……
Heart racing.
Now it's me.
I have handcuffs on and am being led along a tunnel-like corridor.

I'm in what feels like an underground garage and the prison van is waiting.
Breathe.
Walk.
Breathe.
I can't go in there.
I can't go to prison.
I'm at the top of the steps and inside the van are five cubicles on either side. Two of them I know are occupied and I am put into the third. The seat faces forward onto the metal partition in front and to my right is a window. The door is closed until there is just enough room to remove my cuffs. The door is closing. To my left is a small window into the interior of the van. I feel like I am being buried alive.
"George" I told myself "This is the lowest you are ever going to be in your life".
There is more noise outside as the remaining prisoners are put into their pens. Oh god! The engine has started, I'm going to prison.

LINCOLN PRISON

I was in the prison van and fear was like a cork bobbing on a rising tide, swelling up inside me, and what was more frightening was that the situation was completely out of my control. There was a bit of banter between some of the other prisoners, obviously experienced travellers, courtesy of H.M. Prisons. I glanced to my left and the man opposite looked muscular and powerful, wearing his skinhead like a warning. I looked away quickly in case he could sense my eyes upon him and know my fear.

The van slowed and came to a stop at a set of traffic lights. In the car below my window, I could see a woman in the passenger seat looking up. She couldn't see me through the blacked-out windows, but I could see her clearly. I felt ashamed and wished that I was sitting in one of those cars, going nowhere in particular but at least going somewhere. I closed my eyes and tried to pretend that I was in the car beside the woman; the sun was shining, and we could be going to visit her family. I opened my eyes and the car was gone. The man opposite was looking at me, I could sense it. I looked over to acknowledge him and gave him a single nod. He raised his head slightly in reply. We both looked away.

We stopped again and I could see a building through the window, then I could see two huge brown gates. I was terrified and I think that if I had been told that I was going somewhere to be executed I couldn't have felt more afraid than I did in that moment. In a van with five other men and two guards, I felt like I was alone. It was the fear of not having anyone on my side, no-one in my corner, no friends, no family, no-one to care if I lived or died in there and also it was that fear of the unknown.

The brown gates opened, the van drove in and the gates closed behind. This left us in no-mans land with the gates to heaven behind and only a set of railings between us and hell. The railings slid back and the van drove slowly forward into an enclosure, like a huge courtyard with the prison wrapped around it. The van door opened and we were all ushered out, up a staircase and into a holding room on the right at the top of the stairs. The room was already occupied by eight men who I assumed were also prisoners. A gate was closed on us and we all sat quietly. A guard appeared about twenty minutes later and with clipboard in hand he shouted,

"Right, listen up, I will be calling you out in alphabetical order, when your name is called come out and we will get you sorted."

I was taking deep and long breaths but trying to do it without anyone realising. The last thing that I wanted was for any of the others to suspect that I was afraid. I thought that would probably invite trouble.
"Right! First up…Bamby!"
I closed my eyes for a split second in realisation that my name alone was going to invite trouble. The men were laughing and making comments, so I stood up and said,
"Yeah…alright…fucking hell……"
Was I convincing? I had to be convincing. I was hard, didn't care who laughed and in fact maybe they should be wondering who I am.

Well, it seemed to have worked, the comments stopped.
I was marched over to a desk where I had to go through my details: name, address, sentence, did I understand? Then I was asked if I would like to keep my watch on. Instantly, I thought that if I kept my watch then it was just one more thing to worry about and one more thing that someone could want to take from me.
"No"
Would I like to keep my trainers on?
I thought well I really wouldn't care if they took my trainers but at least I know that they are comfortable, and I can run fast in them!
"Yes"
Then I was taken through to the next room.
"Right! Strip off."
Oh god, this is where it starts to get really bad! I've seen this in movies but never expected that I would be playing the starring role. I took my clothes off but left my underpants on.
"Right, underpants off."

I took my pants off, then clasped my hands in front of my genitals. Strange how when men shower together, nudity is familiar and acceptable but when you are naked with two men in uniform are looking on, it is embarrassing and humiliating. I had to go to the hatch in the wall behind me where a pile of clothes was handed out. In the third room, I was allowed to dress, and I sat waiting for the other thirteen intakes.

Someone then came in with trays of food and plastic cutlery. We were given pie, chips and beans and tea was served in a plastic mug. Even though I couldn't remember my last decent meal, it was difficult to eat.

I felt sick. After ten minutes the trays were collected up and we were told to get into single file.
The door opened into a hexagonal area which had corridors leading off in different directions to the prison wings, each with four floors.
I struggled to control the panic that I felt bubbling just beneath the surface.

Oh my god, I am in prison.

The guard opened one of the doors off the hexagon; the sign outside read 'B Wing'.
We walked through and passed a huge bull of a man in a white vest, sitting behind a table. A young, slightly built lad was standing behind, shaving the head of the first guy. The first seven or so cells on the left-hand side were all open and as we passed, the guard yelled,
"Right, first two, in there!" guiding the first two in line into the cell.
"Right, next two, in there!"
"You two, in there!"

That was it, I was in, and with the guy next in line behind me, who by coincidence was the skinhead from the van. The door slammed behind us and now I was alone, in a prison cell, with a scary motherfucker. I was already wondering if the young lad outside was the prison whipping boy.. and what other things he was being made to do as well as head shaving. The scary motherfucker spoke,
"Ya alright mate?"
"Yes, sound. You alright? Fucking hell, what happens now?"
"We just fucking chill out, they're not going to let us out 'til the morning, we're new inmates."
I thought that he had probably been in prison loads of times before. In fact, he had been out on appeal that day, but it had been rejected and he was just returning.
"What you in here for?" he asked.
"I hit a taxi driver."
"Fucking hell, you must have hit him hard to end up here."
I told him the story about jumping bail and then getting re-arrested, then I asked him what he was in for.
"I caught me Mrs shagging the next-door neighbour, so I stabbed him with a garden fork"
He'd been sentenced to three and a half years.

This is it…I'm dead…. bloody typical that I should end up sharing a cell with a psycho.

He said that I would have to have the top bunk, that he couldn't get up there, so I said that was fine and that I preferred that bunk anyway. I'd have had any bunk, slept on the floor, anything, I just didn't want him to kill me.

.

I climbed up onto the bed and he slid onto the bottom bunk. Now I had the chance to look around the cell. There was a stainless-steel sink and toilet, with no seat, a small table, two chairs and a small bin. On the wall, there was a cork noticeboard, empty and waiting for photos and reminders of home. I imagined a picture of Sally and the mountains of New Zealand, and I felt like my heart was being crushed.

About an hour later, there was a clanking of keys, and the door flew open.
"One for you…..one for you!" The guard threw a transparent carrier bag to each of us in turn.

Door closed. Door locked.

Inside the bag was a plastic mug and cutlery; a few sachets of sugar and powdered milk; a few tea bags; toothbrush and toothpaste; a bar of soap; a small bottle of shampoo; a comb; a face flannel; a razor; a roll of toilet paper.

It was about 6pm when we were put into our cells and at 8pm we were allowed out. Mark, the not-quite-so-scary motherfucker, gave me the low-down, so I put a tea bag, sugar and powdered milk in my mug and went with him to the end of corridor where we could get hot water from the geyser. Then we had to go back to our cell.
At 9pm the lights were switched out.

At 7am prompt, the cell door opened, and it was time to get up. We had to queue up with a tray onto which was served a rasher of bacon, an overcooked egg, an undercooked sausage and a few beans. We also had to collect the day's rations of teabags, sugar and powdered milk sachets. These we took back to the cell and then went to the geyser for hot water in our mugs. Then it was back to our cell again for lock-in whilst we ate.

9.30am Induction Course.
We were taken to a room where an information video about AIDS was played for us, and I started to feel that familiar panic returning. An officer told us about the prison rules, then we were called individually into another room. I was faced with three uniformed guards.
"George Bamby....Assault. Yeah, he beat an old pensioner up..."
I reacted instantly,
"I didn't fucking beat an old pensioner up! It was a taxi driver and he was about twenty-five!"
"Aarrrh...just testing ya! You know what you are in here for!"
"Yes"
"...and you know that you are remanded in custody for two weeks, after which time you will be returned to court?"
"Yeah"
"Right...who are you padded up with?"
"Mark Millinschip"
"Right...and are you happy to stay with him?"
"Yeah....sound."
"Right...B32"

He handed me a piece of paper with my name, prison number and release date.
I was taken upstairs to my new cell, B32, which was to be my home for the next two weeks. Mark was already in there. I couldn't tell if he was pleased to see me, I don't suppose that he really cared. I didn't really think about it at the time but if I had asked to move then he would have known about it and maybe I would have had trouble with him.

Half an hour later the door opened.
"Canteen!"
Mark was already on his feet,
"Fucking great!" he said, rubbing his hands together. "This is what ya look forward to."
We were taken to what I thought was the end cell, but in fact it was a shop of sorts with bowls filled with sweets like black jacks and fruit salad. There were bowls of pens, paper, tobacco, Rizlas, lighters and all other sorts of bits. I was still only on my first day inside and I felt like Aladdin on his first trip into the cave.
We had a £10 allowance each. As I had money on me when I was brought in, I at least had a balance to start with, otherwise I wouldn't have been able to buy anything. I bought a couple of ounces of tobacco

and Risla papers, a disposable lighter and a few sweets and went back to my cell. Mark came back in, and I rolled up my first cigarette in a day and a half. I lay on my bunk, and I felt a head rush as the nicotine hit my system. I really should give up smoking I thought for a minute, but that cigarette just tasted too good.

Every day, all the prisoners were allowed two hours out of their cells on 'association'. During this time, we were allowed to go down to play pool or table tennis or watch a movie. There was also a library and a gym. The rest of the time we were all in our cells unless out for breakfast, lunch or tea. I wasn't allowed to get a job as I was on remand and only there for two weeks.

Mark, who I was 'banged up' with, was a stereotypical prison hard case. He knew everyone on the wing as he had already done nine months of his sentence. He had loads of cannabis that his visitors had smuggled in, I know not how! Due to my extensive scar tissue, I was permitted three showers a day as I told the prison doctor that my skin was really dry. Not to pass up an opportunity, Mark recruited me to drop off his cannabis deliveries on my way to the shower block, in exchange for phone cards and tobacco. I never got any hassle from anyone because of this, so my two weeks passed without incident. All the men in there seemed to be just doing their time and getting through each day.

Two weeks later, I packed my bag and was led out of my cell on the way back to court. There were shouts of,
"Good luck George!"
"You'll be sound, you won't be back here!"
and as I left, I really felt like I needed some good luck. I hoped that I would never have to see the inside of a prison ever again.

Back to court.
I was given a month for the assault charge and a month for the breach of bail: two months in prison! For good behaviour, I was told that I would have to do one month, which meant that I had to go back to prison for another two weeks.

I was put in a reception cell for the night and the following morning I asked the guards if it would be possible to go back to the same cell. 'Better the devil you know', was along the lines of my thinking process. They put me back in B32 and I felt relieved. Mark was not the scary motherfucker anymore and I suppose in that month we were friends. We made plans for his release day that I would pick him up and we'd go to Skegness and get drunk! However, when I was released after two weeks, I just wanted to get as far away from there as possible, to put it behind me and never have to think about it again. So, I wasn't there when Mark was released, but I'm sure by then he would have made other plans with other inmates. If he made it to Skegness though, I hope he had a great day and had that drink, and I also hope that was his last stretch inside and that he turned his life around. For me, one time was enough, well more than enough, but I did my time and counted it as a lesson and a once in a lifetime experience.

On the day of my release, I was up early and raring to go. The cell hatch opened, and the duty officer told me to pack my stuff up and get ready to leave. At half eight, the cell door swung open, and I knew that I was on my way. Soon I could put all of it behind me. I had time to say a quick goodbye to Mark and then I was taken to the release room where I changed out of my prison clothes and put my old familiar stuff back on. I was allowed to have a shower and as the water ran over my face, I imagined that all my worries were washing away: gone was the despair; gone was the desperation; gone was the feeling of injustice; gone was the fear. It was no use wasting a minute more thinking about what had happened. It was over and done with, a memory. Any thoughts spent on regrets would be a waste of time when I could be enjoying the here and now.

I left prison with no money. The little I had was stuck over in an account in New Zealand. I was given a discharge grant of £72 in the form of a giro, and a rail ticket. I didn't have a clue where I should get the train to. I suppose that Manchester would have been the obvious choice but in fact it was the last place on earth where I wanted to be. I had a friend, Matt Robinson, who had been over to New Zealand for a year playing football for the New Plymouth Rangers. He lived in Oxford so that seemed like as good a destination as any.

There were four prisoners up for release that day. We were all walked down together, along the corridors, through the main reception, into the open yard area and through the large gates. Then we stood behind the solid brown gates, just them between us and the rest of the world. A door was opened to allow us out into the street beyond.

“Thanks for coming. Next time you come, bring a friend.” Was the cheery departing quip from the guard.

The things that we all take for granted are the things that are most important to us. We don’t appreciate the value of freedom until it is taken away from us. As I walked out onto the street, the cars… silver, white, blue, red, van…motorbike…all people going about their lives, people with choices and decisions to make. The trees and the birds were beautiful, things that I never imagined that I would miss. I glanced back at the brown door and knew for sure that I would never be going through that door again, not ever in my life.

OXFORD OR BUST

I walked down the road with one of the other lads that had been released and we went into the Post Office where I cashed my £72 giro and then we went over to the train station. The lad said that he was going to the off-licence for beer, but I just wanted to get on my way. Whilst I was waiting for my train, I went into the licensed café on the platform and had a pint of lager. It was the best-tasting pint that I have ever had because it had the taste of freedom. I can't imagine being locked up for years and for people that say that prison is a soft option and not a deterrent, I would say, go and try it!

I phoned Matt and he said that I was welcome to go and stay with him, so half an hour later I was on a train racing towards Nottingham to collect my belongings from the police station.

I had two suitcases, sealed in plastic, waiting for me. The officers on duty were very sympathetic to what had happened to me and made me a cup of tea. They said that they couldn't believe that I had been sent to prison, that people get off with doing a lot worse and they wished me luck as I went on my way to Nottingham train station.

Once in Oxford, I got a taxi to Matt's house and was relieved when he opened the door and threw his arms around me. He was genuinely pleased to see me and at least I knew that I could get a few good nights' sleep and decide where to go from there.

Matt was sharing with his girlfriend, Georgina, and a black lad, to whom I apologise for not being able to remember his name. They were all students and Matt had explained the circumstances as to how I had been sent to prison for a month and they welcomed me and agreed that I could stay for as long as I liked. My rent would save them all a bit of money each week. I went upstairs and put my bags in my room and then I sat at the kitchen table with Matt and announced,
"Right, I have to get a job."

The next morning, I got up early and walked down into the town. Whilst locked up I had been thinking about my life and about Sally and I knew that I wanted her with me, wherever I was. I rang her from a payphone, and I told her that I loved her and asked her to come over to England. I would never be allowed to return to New Zealand, so I knew that it was a lot to ask of her. She agreed to come but she said that she didn't have the money, so I told her that I would get the cash together as soon as I could.

Now I had a driving force behind me. Sally would not be able to come over unless I got a job. I didn't have any money behind me to enable me to set up a business, so I walked the streets in search of work. I went into shops, bars, cafés and restaurants. Then, having been turned away from one shop, I saw a restaurant across the road with a sign in the window. 'staff vacancy', so I went inside and was told that there was a job going in the kitchen. That day I started work as the KP/ kitchen porter/pot washer on £6 an hour.

My working day started at 7am, washing down the kitchen. I worked as many hours as I could, every day. I got on well with the manager and I said that I wanted to earn as much money as I could and so any extra hours he had were given to me. They were long, hard days and I was more tired than I could ever remember being whilst at work. Since being in the children's home and enduring washing the pots as a punishment, I have hated washing up. I hated it then and I hate it now. I worked from 7am to 3pm and then I continued onto the next shift which ran from 3pm until midnight. Before long I was moved from 'the pots' to food preparation. Within a couple of weeks, I was cooking pizzas and pasta which were the mainstay of the menu. I saved every penny that I could, drinking and eating only when I was at work, and I smoked roll-ups to save money on cigarettes. After three weeks of working seven days a week, seventeen hours a day, I had saved up about £1200. At last, I could send the money over for Sally and it was that light at the end of the tunnel that had kept me going through those dark days.

I carried on working and saving until finally the day came when Sally was due to arrive. By then I had paid a deposit on a furnished rental flat, although there wasn't much in it in the way of furniture. I had bought a few basic necessities and at least it was a start. I went down to Heathrow Airport to meet her and brought her back to Oxford.

I knew that things would have to change as I didn't want to be working all the hours that I had been doing. My relationship with Sally was far too precious and I knew that I had to spend time with her if things were going to work out. Although she was happy to be with me, the dark cloud overhead was that she had left her two children behind in New Zealand. She had split up from her husband to be with me when we were both over there, and the law had given custody to him due to his ability financially to provide for them. Access to the children was made difficult due to the circumstances under which the relationship had broken down. He was resentful and used the children to punish her. The outcome was that Sally became very depressed and I think that when I rang and gave her the opportunity of making a fresh start with me, she thought that it would be better for the children rather than being in the middle of the constant battle over access.

Sally and I strolled hand in hand around Oxford town centre. It was a beautiful sunny day, and the architecture is so overpowering and magnificent that all our worries paled into insignificance, and we just revelled in being back together. The streets were buzzing with tourists of all nationalities and students on bicycles wove their way from campus to campus to halls of residence. It seemed so cosmopolitan and so unlike Manchester and this was the first time since I arrived there that I had had the opportunity to enjoy it.

The Tourist Office caught my eye, primarily because of the human traffic passing through its door. I dragged Sally inside to join the throng searching through leaflets and bombarding the staff with questions. I couldn't believe how busy it was and my nose for an opportunity began to twitch. Sally was quite happy to go off browsing the shops and sights for an hour which gave me the chance to do some research. I asked one of the guys behind the counter what time he was due to finish as I wanted to meet up for a coffee and ask him a few questions about Oxford. Even though it was an odd request, he said that he was finishing at midday. I didn't care that he was obviously gay and probably thought that I was making a lunch date. I am not homophobic so planned to just be my charming self and I wasn't worried that he might be disappointed to find out that I was straight. You win some, you lose some, but at least I could pick his brains for an hour. I met him; he was a great guy. I bought coffees and sandwiches and we chatted about Oxford. I discovered the majority of tourists are French, German and Spanish, with a small percentage of Americans and Chinese. I asked him about the sales in the Tourist Office. In fact, I spent an hour draining information from him which I could then pump into my next venture.

An hour later I met up with Sally.
"I'm going to start a business!"

OXFORD TOURISM GUIDE

That afternoon I bought a second-hand computer that was advertised in the local paper. It only cost £100 so it was a good bit of capital investment to set me on my way. Then I went to the local library and loaned some software, and I collected all the leaflets that they had there: publicity material from hotels, businesses and places of interest.

Later, I sat down at home and listed all the top restaurants, nightclubs, cinemas and tourist attractions. Then I collated emergency and information telephone numbers including the Spanish, German and French Embassies. By the time that I had finished I had about four A4 pages of information. Now I was ready to really set to work.

I produced the Oxford Tourism Guide. On the front I put an index of such things as 'accommodation', 'places to eat', 'places to go' and 'colleges to visit'. I had the first four pages in English, the next four in French, then Spanish, then German. I utilised the fantastic local student population to get my translations done. I am always enterprising if nothing else!

I set the price at £2 which was displayed on the front, and I went off to a local shop to get my first one hundred copies photocopied! Then armed with my publication, I went to the Council Offices and said that I wanted to set up a booth outside the Tourism Office to sell my pamphlets.
"Ooooh, you can't do that!"
Red tape and bureaucratic diarrhoea spilled out.
Obstacles, always obstacles! BUT… obstacles are put there to climb so I donned my helmet and ropes and set off for the summit.

I found out that in the 1800s there was a law under which I could still apply for a 'Pedlars' Licence'. As this law had not been revoked, it meant that I could apply to the Police for the princely sum of £5 to enable me to 'peddle my wares' on the public thoroughfare. I duly completed the form giving details of my trade, supplied my two passport-sized photographs (the law had obviously been reviewed at least once then since 1890 or whenever it was!) and once it was stamped and approved, I was in business. Times had changed since the days of selling fruit from a hand-woven basket, but the law remained the same: as long as I didn't remain in the same place for longer than ten minutes then I was operating within the parameters of my licence.

I had a tabard made up which read 'Oxford Tourism Guide' and then underneath it said "£2", and for my first ten minutes I stood outside the Tourist Office, defiant to the end as always. I had a bag over my shoulder with my first one hundred copies burning a hole in it. It wasn't long before I had £200 in my hand and was off to get more photocopied. Before I knew it, I had sold four hundred and was planning on how to get them reproduced more cheaply and in larger quantities.

I had 10,000 copies printed and recruited Sally, Matt and another guy to the sales team. Matt and his flatmate had just finished college for the summer holidays, so it was a great opportunity for them to earn some extra cash. The four of us headed for the main tourist attractions and with the seemingly endless supply we now had at the flat, business was booming. We were selling on average about two hundred guides a day and taking into account the 50p each copy that I was paying my 'employees' and the 50p a copy it was costing to produce, I was still making a tidy profit. I was making in excess of £1,000 a week.

When the college holidays were over, the weather started to get worse, and the numbers of tourists was dwindling. By this time, I had saved almost £10,000 and I'd paid for Sally to have a holiday in New Zealand to visit her family. Whilst she was away, I was thinking about our life at the opposite end of the earth and about the difference in lifestyles and cultures. By the time she got back I was totally dissatisfied with living in England and was itching to move on.

Flicking through the local 'Advertiser' I saw a campervan for sale for £6,000. I phoned immediately and went over to see the vendor. It was a fantastic vehicle for the money, with a double bed plus two singles, a shower unit, kitchen equipment and stereo. I think the words that I used to Sally were,
"Let's fuck off from this god-forsaken shit-hole and travel around Europe!"
Surprisingly she didn't want to leave. She had just got a job working on a market stall and was settling into life in England. I felt trapped and said that I was going to leave and after much coercion on my part, she finally agreed to go with me.

That was it, I rang the man who had the campervan for sale and went round to see him. I offered him £4,000 and when he refused, I asked him what was the least that he would accept. He insisted that he wanted

£6,000 before he would part with it. I left without making a deal, but my negotiations were far from over. On my first visit he had said that he drank every night in a particular pub in Whitney. This gave me two pieces of information: the first that he liked a drink and the second, where I could find him. A few evenings later, I took Sally to Whitney and we went into his local public house. Sure enough, an hour later, the man with the van arrived and ordered his first pint. I asked him if he still had his campervan for sale, guessing that he would have. He said that he did.
Great! Everything was going to plan so far.
Right, this was it, in for the kill.
"Look mate, I really liked the van, but I can't meet that price, I can give you four and a half grand for it....cash...tonight."
"What?....Cash?...Tonight?"
The fish was nibbling the bait.
"Yes mate.,..cash..in readies...tonight."
He was thinking.
The fish was on the hook.
"Aww...let me just have a think"
Ten minutes later.
"Right...let's do it!...You can have it for four and a half grand."

I got a taxi back to my flat where I had a stash of cash and then went onto his house where I paid him, and we completed the paperwork. I'd had a couple of drinks, so Sally drove the van back to our flat where we opened a bottle of wine and chatted about where we could go. I lit a cigarette and walked over to the window. Below, the campervan on the drive was illuminated by the dull glow from the overhead streetlight. I was excited and felt the pace of my heart quicken at the thought of a new adventure about to start. I turned back to Sally,
"We're going tomorrow!"
She knew me well enough to know that I wasn't joking, so she started packing.

FUCK IT, WE'LL JUST DRIVE!
"Where are we going?" Sally, unlike me, needed some sort of structure to her life.
"Fuck it, we'll just drive," meant I didn't have a clue; it just depended where the road led.

I took the bare minimum with me. Due to the nomadic life that I had led so far, I had never got attached to material things and I was not burdened by sentimentality. The only reminders that I had from my childhood were three photographs taken during my time with Wes and Dee. Sally didn't have a lot of things either because she had been in England for such a short time.

We drove to one of the southern ports, I can't remember exactly which one now, but I think it may have been Portsmouth. From my preliminary enquiries, I knew that we could get a ferry to Bilbao in northern Spain. Unbeknown to Sally, I didn't have a driving licence, I didn't have insurance on the van and the tax had just run out. These small details were not about to worry me, and it was better if she didn't know.

The ferry cost about £200 and the trip took approximately twelve hours. It was an overnight ferry and when we went upstairs to the bar, the atmosphere was good: People were drinking, and everyone onboard seemed to be in good spirits. We joined in the party and drank to our future together. Later, we got a cabin and managed to sleep for a few hours, so with everything considered it was a great start to our travels.
As we approached Bilbao we stood on the stern of the ship and looked forward to the port. It was an industrial landscape, littered with vast containers and rusting vessels, cranes and grey buildings. It was not the welcome we had expected.
"What a shit hole!" was the only comment that I could muster.
Sally looked downtrodden and disappointed.
We rallied round, making jokes, and my optimism was enough for both of us. It wasn't long before Sally was smiling again and we disembarked, drove through passport control and were on our way.

Before long we saw a sign marked 'Madrid' and that seemed as good a place as any to head for.
The roads were long and Romanesque; we could see for miles ahead….nothing. The landscape was bleak and unstimulating. After a

couple of hours, we stopped and made a cup of tea as we had stocked up on supplies before we left Oxford. Then we drove on….then stopped off again for tea and a bacon sandwich. We were like cub scouts on their first jamboree. Madrid was getting nearer, 100 kilometres, 80 kilometres, 40, *10.....oh my god!*
What lane are we supposed to be in?
What side of the road are we on?
All this traffic!
What did that signpost say!?
Are you reading the signs, Sally!!?
Car lanes, bike lanes, bus lanes.
How big is this city?
Where are we now?
From the desolation of the roads on the way, suddenly there was an explosion of traffic.
We just kept driving; we may have driven around the city three times and through it twice; we didn't have a clue where we were or which direction we were heading.

Finally, the madness ejected us back to normality and the roads became quieter, narrower, less lanes with fewer cars.
We pulled into a service station, drew the curtains, locked the doors, and climbed into bed.

The next day we were up with the first sounds of morning. People and cars started to disturb the quietness of the night. As the sky lightened, we both showered and got ready for the day ahead. We headed south, not deliberately, but that was the way that fate sent us.

After hours and hours of driving we started seeing signs for Malaga and I began to feel optimistic. Although we hadn't really discussed where we were planning to end up, I was beginning to feel that we were coming to the end of our journey. The landscape became more agreeable and the towns we passed through were getting bigger. From villages that seemed to sell nothing but Spanish pottery, and the acres and acres of plastic cloches shielding their secret crops from the insects, birds and sun, we now saw shops and restaurants. We were back in civilisation.

Soon the signs and the sights became more exciting. The coastline was magnificent and with the windows open and the breeze blowing through the cab, it was a far cry from the cold, wet weather that we had left behind in England. Blue skies stretched to infinity and white villages beckoned from the hills, but we kept on driving south. Torremolinos…Fuengirola….Benalmadena.

We drove through the centre of Marbella and, as we stopped in the traffic, the sound of water to my left drew my attention to a large ornate fountain in a park. It had two tiers and on the bottom wall four tourists sat eating ice creams. I found out later that this is the Fuente Virgen del Rocio which is in the centre of the Parque de Alameda. The edges of it are tiled with emblems and pictures.

The walkway through the park looked like marble, streets paved with gold, and it reminded me of that old story about Dick Whittington who went off to London in search of wealth. There were benches the length of the park but the ones close to the fountain were solidly and squarely built and tiled in white with blue edging. The backs were ornate and displayed pictures of unfamiliar buildings. The foliage in the park was exotic with huge palms giving shade to the Spanish families beneath. Their children danced around, with tanned faces decorated with smiles. It was a far cry from England.

A horse-drawn carriage passed by on the opposite side of the road, its red wheels matched the interior of the hood, and the horse was immaculately groomed. A couple sat in the back, the man with his arm placed protectively around the shoulders of his blonde companion.

The breathtaking backdrop to Marbella is mountainous, the grey craggy horizon rising majestically against the unblemished blue sky. The roads were busy, and I think by then we were in three lanes of traffic. Ahead, a huge spire projected from a block of marble in the middle of a small roundabout. The main body of the spire was made of what looked like copper and it was topped with a point of glass. I now know this to be Marbella's 'Piruli' but I don't know anything about its history or what significance, if any, it has.

As we left Marbella, we passed under the now famous white arch with the name of the city carved in huge letters. Still we drove on, bypassing, for now at least, Puerto Banus with its flamboyant show of wealth, yachts and cruisers lining the port. As we continued, we saw signs for Estepona and Algeciras and then one sign jumped out. That was it! We were going to Gibraltar!

GIBRALTAR

As we drove along the seafront in La Linea, the Spanish town which borders with British Gibraltar, we could see the Rock rising out of the sea in the distance. The main bulk of the country looked to be uninhabitable with the whole population clustered in the buildings which skirted this rocky peninsular. A sandy isthmus links Gibraltar to Spain and it is over this area that the territorial arguments centre. As we got nearer, we could see that there were areas of the rock covered in greenery and other parts where the white limestone was exposed to the erosion of the climate.

The north face is pierced with man-made holes in a horizontal line, barely discernible amongst the shadows. These I later learned were the openings from the Great Seige Tunnels. During the war of American Independence, France and Spain had combined in an attempt to recapture the Rock from the British. This was the 14th Great Seige and it lasted from July 1779 to February 1783. The Governor of Gibraltar at the time was a man called General Eliot and it is reported that he offered a reward to anyone that could suggest a means of mounting a gun on a projection from the northern face of the Rock, known as 'the notch'. A Sergeant Major Ince put forward the idea of tunnelling through the rock and subsequently work started on May 25th in 1782. Eighteen men set to work with sledgehammers, crowbars and dynamite. The dust and fumes were overpowering, so a decision was made to open a vent to admit air into the tunnel. It was immediately obvious that the aperture provided an excellent vantage point for a gun and the first one was mounted. By the time the siege ended there were four guns in position and the tunnel was an impressive three hundred and seventy feet in length. Work did not stop there though as the Royal Engineers went on to tunnel two further galleries. If you get the opportunity to visit the Seige Tunnels in Gibraltar, take a moment to appreciate the possibilities that can come from one innovative idea and plenty of determination and hard work. That is the mantra by which I live my life and the second one is that it is better to have tried and failed than to never have tried.

I pulled over at the side of the road.
"You'd better drive" I suggested.
"Why?"
"I don't have a driving licence."
"What do you mean, you don't have a driving licence?"

"I mean…I don't have a driving licence, just swap seats, come on we are here now."
Sally had her licence from New Zealand, but we didn't need it anyway. We passed through the border showing only our passports and that was it, we were in! I later found out that if I had been stopped in Spain without documentation, the vehicle would have been impounded and if I had failed to produce them at a future date then my campervan would have been destroyed. We had been very lucky to have got that far.
"You only wanted me to come to drive you over the border!" Sally was not happy, and it was not a good start to our new life.

We enjoyed the first few days, sleeping in the van at Europa Point. From here we could see both Spain across the bay and North Africa across the Straits. On a clear day it was possible to see the buildings in Ceuta which is a Spanish enclave on the North African coast. There was a small, solitary shop near where we parked up, which bore a sign above the door: 'THE LAST SHOP IN EUROPE, MUCH CHEAPNESS'. When I met the proprietor, Michael Faria, I realised that it was a reflection of his sense of humour combined with his conviction that the wording was a good marketing ploy to make his shop memorable. The sign presented a great photo opportunity for visiting tourists and the bus loads that visited Europa Point all poured into his shop to buy ice creams and souvenirs.

As usual I made conversation with everyone that Sally and I bumped into. I was particularly interested in finding a newspaper or magazine that might include flat rentals and the second-hand sale of furniture. We were on a tight budget, but we couldn't stay in the campervan indefinitely. The consensus of opinion was that the only publication which covered this area was the Gibraltar Chronicle. I bought a copy immediately and noted from the top that it was published daily. The classified adverts in the back were very limited and on the day that I purchased a copy, there were only seven items listed. Two of them were for 'lost and found', someone had found a cat, and another had lost a gold ring. I was amazed and pushed my informant further.
"Surely there must be somewhere that you can advertise things. How would you go about selling a sofa for instance?"
"Oh yes, there is." He was happy at last to be able to help. "Safeways!"

Sally and I piled into the van and set off for the superstore, which was on the west side of the Rock, on an area of reclaimed land.

Inside the entrance, on the right, there was a cafeteria, and I was amazed to see that it was licensed. Men were sitting at the bar sipping beer whilst their wives or partners shopped. Ideal! What could be better? I hate food shopping at the best of times and only do it out of necessity. If someone else will do it for me then I am happy to let them. I am happily chauvinistic in my approach to life, and I have upset many women over the years with my opinions and comments.

Sally and I sat and had breakfast. The morning sun was hot, so we were glad to be in the cool interior of the supermarket. I looked over at the men at the bar. Would I want to drink a beer in the morning? Well, I could probably force one down if it was as hot as this and Sally was shopping. Sally was looking at me.
"What?" I asked, guilty in the knowledge that I had already mapped out our next visit to the supermarket.
"I asked if you had finished." Sally said, oblivious to the fact that I was planning to land her with the food shopping from here on in.
"Yes, come on, let's go and have a look at these boards."

There were about eight huge notice boards covered with cards, advertising things for sale, services, pets, lost and found….and there was one card for a flat to rent. I had been warned that finding rental accommodation in Gibraltar is very difficult, so I rang the number on the card straight away and arranged to meet up with the advertiser.

He took me in his car, and we drove out of the town, south, and then up the hill, past the casino.
I wondered where on earth his flat was. Then we turned right and headed down a hill. I could see the bay and Algeciras across the water. We passed between two tall buildings, the sun hidden from view, and the coolness of the shade was a pleasant release from the midday heat. He pulled over.
"This is it, here we are."
A green and white building stood to my right. It didn't look very inviting. There was a small bar further along the road and through the window I could see two men playing a game of pool. Another stood in the door, smoking a cigarette.

The marble entrance to the flats had seen years of usage but it was clean and smelled fresh.
"It's on the top floor"

I looked around for a lift but there wasn't one. We started up the marble staircase and five floors later, we finally arrived at the flat.

I remember the building being so cool. Outside the heat was almost unbearable and due to my scar tissue and my inability to sweat, I was suffering more than most.

The wooden door to the flat swung open and we walked into the cool interior.
Marble floors!
It looked good.
The rooms were enormous and there was a huge terrace which had fantastic views over the bay. I fell in love with the place straight away and immediately paid him a month's deposit and a month's rent in advance. I agreed to set up a direct debit to pay £400 monthly after that and I was ecstatic that I had found somewhere so soon and that it was a great place, furnished, and with views. I thought that Sally would be overjoyed but although she liked the flat, after a couple of days she told me that she hated Gibraltar and didn't want to stay. I hoped that she would have a change of heart and thought that maybe once I'd established myself in a job or a business that she would see things differently. I asked her to give it a bit of time.

GIBRALTAR EXCHANGE AND MART

A couple of days later I woke up with a plan. I do some of my most productive thinking when I am on the toilet but on that occasion, I think my brain must have been in overdrive and as the morning dawned, another business idea saw the light of day.

I jumped into the campervan and drove down to Safeways. Scouring the noticeboards, I saw an advertisement for a second-hand computer. It was about £150 so I made a call and within half an hour I had paid for it and loaded it into the back of the van. I took it back to the flat and once I'd managed to sort out all the cables, I set it up on the table. I still had the computer software from the Oxford tourism guide, so I installed that. I was on my way to publishing my first magazine.

My first idea had been to print a newspaper, but I realised that the Gibraltar Chronicle had that area of the market pretty much sewn up and as it was published daily would be impossible to compete with. My second idea then, and the one upon which I was focussing my attention, was to produce a magazine where residents could buy and sell.

I rang the Gibraltar Chronicle and asked to place an advert to say that I would advertise, for free, anything that people wanted to buy or sell. They refused to take my advert on the grounds that it represented competition to their own business. I never take a defeat lying down. If there is a way around an obstacle, I will do my utmost to find it; If there isn't a way around it, I will dig my way through it!

I returned once more to Safeways, this time armed with an A4 pad of lined paper. I bypassed the bar cafeteria and went straight to the noticeboards, where I stood and copied every single detail from every single card on the wall.

Pushchair for sale, how much they brought it for, how much they wanted....price...phone number..daytime...evening.

After two hours I went into the cafeteria and had a coffee, flicking through my pad and very happy with the way it was going....but what a job it was...I still had over half of the boards to go. With the coffee finished, I could delay getting back to the task in hand no longer. I went back to the noticeboards. About half an hour later a security guard walked over.

"Excuse me...what are you doing?"

"What do you mean, what am I doing?" I was tired and irritable by this time.
"Well, you've been standing here for hours and writing…what are you doing? What's going on?"
"I'm copying all of the adverts off the cards." It was the truth.
"What for?" he asked authoritatively, puffing out his chest beneath his uniform, trying to demand my respect.
"What the fuck has it got to do with you?" He didn't have it. Respect has to be earned.
"I'm Security" he said as if that would bring me to my knees.
I said, "I don't give a fuck who you are, there's nothing to say I can't copy all the adverts."
"Well, what are you doing that for?" his face had softened into the inquisitive features of a cat chasing a ball of string. He was harmless and probably bored.
I told him that it was a business idea and that I wasn't doing any harm. Satisfied that I presented no threat to shoppers, staff or national security, he became my ally and returned every half hour for a status report and a chat.

I had been to the local telephone offices and paid my £100 deposit to have a phone line connected in the flat. I just needed to sort out an internet service which I did without any problems. Then for the next three days, I locked myself in the flat and I telephoned the numbers on every single advert that I had copied from Safeways.
"Hello, do you still have your pushchair for sale?"
"Yes."
"I'm starting a new magazine and I'm going to put an advert in for you."
"Oh, and how much does that cost?"
"It's free for you to advertise, it's not going to cost you anything."
"How can that be? It must cost something. Why would you be doing that for us?"

It took me ages to get people to understand that they didn't have to pay for their adverts. Many of them thought that there must be some sort of con involved and some of them could just not grasp the concept of what I was doing, failing to understand how it was possible for me to advertise something for them but not charge them. Eventually however, I had rung all five hundred of the contacts on my list. Items that had already been sold I eliminated, and finally I had about three hundred and ninety adverts to work with. Once I had categorised everything: mother and baby, household appliances, furniture, cars etc., I then set about typing everything into my template. I left plenty of spaces around the classified adverts for my display ads. These ranged in size from one that was the size of a cigarette box to quarter page, half page and full page. I printed everything off and compiled it into a booklet to make my first edition which was to have twelve pages.

Armed with my selling tool, I started at one end of Main Street and walked the full length, going into every shop and business on the way and talking to all the managers. Then I crossed over the road, and I did the same going back up the other way. Once I'd done that, I ventured into the side streets. If you are familiar with Gibraltar and more importantly with the people, then you will know that they are in general very amenable and approachable, and I can say that every person that I spoke to gave me the opportunity to explain what I was doing. If I had tried similar tactics in the UK, I know that I would have had a different reception and that many would have insisted on appointments.

In the 'Car' section, I sold advertising space to car dealers of both new and second-hand cars, driving instructors, mechanics and car hire companies. In the 'Mother and Child' section, I sold to children's clothes and accessories shops. In the 'Ice' section, I sold to Eskimos, well that was soon the joke anyway!

I phoned the Gibraltar telephone company and requested a second line be installed in my flat. This was a continuous ansaphone service, asking classified advertisers to leave details with a phone number and saying that their item would be included in the next week's edition.

On the front cover of my first edition, I plastered the telephone number and the important information that I wanted all the readers to know: that it was free to advertise as long as it was a private sale. There was a separate price list for retail advertisers. I priced the magazine up at £2 a copy and then I approached five newspaper retailers, two shops and three kiosks, and asked them to sell them on sale or return. For the ones that they sold they were to keep £1 per copy, the other £1 I would collect when I picked up the returns. Even though all the outlets had ordered twenty-five copies, on my first print run I did two hundred and fifty and I took fifty to each shop and dropped them off. I gave them each a poster and I stipulated that my magazine be located next to the till, on the counter. It was in their interest to sell the copies as the profit margin on them was higher than on any of the other magazines and newspapers, so all of them agreed. Within two days, all five of the retailers had sold out and were on the phone requesting more copies. The Gibraltar Exchange and Mart was a success!

The second week, I printed a thousand copies, and I left a hundred with each outlet. Some needed more than the hundred and they were all getting orders for the next week's copy. I was selling between seven and eight hundred every week which was great for the shops and fantastic for me because on top of that I was also selling the advertising space. For anyone buying or selling anything, the 'Gibraltar Exchange and Mart' became the magazine to buy and the magazine to advertise in. At last, I thought, I am onto a winner...........hold that thought!

Sally was not happy. I was working non-stop to get the business up and running and she could only see the negative side of everything. She was homesick and missing her children. She hated Gibraltar. She didn't like me working all the time and she moaned and moaned and moaned. The day before her birthday I bought her a one-way flight ticket to New Zealand and put it in with her birthday card. That was the end of our relationship. Sally left and I threw myself back into my work.

I thrive on a challenge, and I give one hundred and ten percent to everything that I start. I was working on average about fifteen hours every day: I was selling the advertising; laying out the copy; phoning every single classified advertiser, every week, to find out if items had been sold; I had to put in the new ads from the 'hot line'....the work was non-stop, and as soon as one edition was out of the way, then the next one was on the horizon.

At this point, I was photocopying all the copies, which was costing over a thousand pounds for every edition, so finding a printer was a priority. The Gibraltar Chronicle newspaper would not print it for me as I was not charging for my classified adverts and consequently their paid ads had declined. There was another publication, 'Gibsport', printed weekly, which primarily as the name implies, reported on the sporting events and achievements of local teams and clubs. They agreed to print my magazine for £450 per edition but due to the popularity and increased circulation of my publication, they soon found that they too were losing advertisers.

The owner of the printing company called me into the office and asked that I refuse adverts from people that were advertising with them and in return he would continue to print my magazine. I think that there was quite a bit of swearing done on my part and our business arrangement ended there and then. I had wanted to use a local printer, but I knew that in order to stop the same thing happening again, I would have to get my printing done over the border in Spain. The same day I arranged to get my copies printed in La Linea, the closest Spanish town. The local printer was disgruntled, not only had he lost his contract for my printing, but I was still going to be approaching his advertisers. Gibraltar is a very small country, covering an area of only 5.8 square miles, the majority of which land is uninhabited. The population is multi-racial and multi-cultural, generally living harmoniously. The Gibraltarians are a close-knit community and faced with an invasion from the outside they can close ranks and present an almost impenetrable defensive front. My printer saw me as an invading enemy and he gathered troops, speaking to all his local contacts which resulted in my advertising sales being affected.

In June 1876, in the eastern Montana territory of America near the Little Bighorn River, the Lakota-Northern Cheyenne, native Americans, annihilated the 7th cavalry of the US Army led by Lieutenant Colonel Custer. The lesson? Know when you are outnumbered and defeated…
Well maybe I was not defeated, not quite, not yet.
I had to turn the tide that was swelling against me and find a chink in the armour that would enable me to regain the confidence of the local population.

That came in the form of Steven Oliveras, a local man and proprietor of a courier company that advertised regularly in my magazine. We got on well and I saw in him the same entrepreneurial spirit that I had. He was forever looking at new business ideas as his own business was already established. After a few negotiations, I sold him forty-nine percent of the Gibraltar Exchange and Mart for £15,000. The agreement was that I would transfer the business from my flat to his office and that his wife, who was already working there, would answer our company phone. His company couriers would collect any artwork from the advertisers, Steven would design the layout and his wife would type out the classifieds. It meant that I had time to speak to advertisers and I lined up twelve-month contracts with many of them.

Just selling a one-page advert for a year was potentially £15,000 in revenue but Steven was not happy and became more and more dissatisfied with the amount of time that I was spending, or rather NOT spending, in the office. As far as I was concerned, I had spent almost a year building up the magazine and now I didn't have to work fifteen hours a day to get the publication out. That was one of the reasons that I had sold almost half of the business. Familiarity breeds contempt and the resentment that Steven felt towards me built up. I didn't help things by spending hours playing pool.

Finally, Steven threatened to use his local contacts to bring the company down by stopping the advertisers. He said he would then restart a similar magazine from scratch. By this time, I was sick and tired of the arguments and threats, and I asked him to buy out my fifty-one percent of the business. We agreed a lump sum, a monthly remuneration for the next year and that the company pay off the finance on my jeep. I was happy to be out of it but sad that I had lost a friend. I told myself that it would be the last time that I took on a partner. I never learn!

STEVE DAVIS

With my business worries out of the way, I was free to party and enjoy life and I did it in style. I was out drinking and playing pool every night. I joined a league and entered all the ranking tournaments. Within a month or so I was the number one ranked player in Gibraltar, and I was selected for the national squad. The team went over to the UK to compete in the World Pool Championships. I won sixty-eight percent of all the games that I played, which was the highest Gibraltarian record. We played against England, Wales, Ireland, France, Belgium and Australia. I loved every minute of it and our team really knew how to have a good time.

Back at home, we all met up for pool at every opportunity and my trophies were accumulating. I was really enjoying life and for a year at least I knew that I didn't have to worry about earning a living.

Whilst I was over in the UK for the World Pool Championships, I made some excellent contacts. I have a naturally extrovert character, I love being the centre of attention and I just love talking to people. There are so many interesting things that you can find out from having a simple conversation and communication opens doors. The one person that you think is insignificant or uninteresting could be a link to an exciting opportunity and every single person I have ever met in my life has at least one funny story to tell.

This time was no different from any other. I was playing pool for Gibraltar but talking for England! During one conversation with someone I met over there, I managed to get the telephone number for Steve Davis, the snooker player. My brain was ticking, after resting for weeks and weeks and the mention of one of my idols had kick-started my business head. I can plan, design a strategy for implementation, and calculate a rough budget instantaneously. Instant business plan! At the mere mention of Steve Davis' name, I had already decided to put on a pool exhibition in Gibraltar.

By this time, I had moved from my flat out of town and was living more centrally, sharing with a woman that I had met through the pool association. Linda Alverez is a great person and we got on really well. She was a fantastic organiser, and she dedicated her time to help me bring to fruition my plans to put on the best eight-ball pool event that Gibraltar had ever seen.

I went to see the owner of a large building near the runway. Until quite recently it had been a Tesco supermarket but now it stood empty and as far as I was concerned it was an ideal place to put on an exhibition. The floor space downstairs was extensive, upstairs there was an area where I could set up a bar, and it had a car park. I agreed a price of £500 for one evening's hire.

I rang Steve Davis and sorted out a date and booked him for the event. Once I had sorted out my celebrity and the venue, I went to the local swimming association and the sports stadium, and I hired their portable tiered seating. I got sponsorship by selling advertising boards around the arena. I included tickets to the event as an incentive for the local companies and with my contacts from the Exchange and Mart I had no problems. I sold about twenty boards at four hundred pounds each which gave me three hundred and fifty profit, on each one. I printed a programme and sold advertising space in that. Then I put the tickets on sale at £15 each. The venue was limited to a capacity of five hundred and within two and half days it was sold out. The local airline, Gibraltar Airways, sponsored the flight for Steve Davis and a local hotel sponsored the accommodation.

It was summer 1999 and life was good. I had two really good friends with whom I did most of my socialising at this time. They were cousins: Jimmy and Leslie Bruzon, and we had a riot every time we went out. Gibraltar is a small place where everyone knows each other, and the local people are amongst the friendliest that I have ever met anywhere on my travels.

In the pool league we played in different bars every week and we also played up the coast in Spain. In a small community the nightlife can be fantastic as you never have to worry about going out on your own. You know people everywhere that you go and it's safe to get home at the end of the night even if you are completely bladdered!

Leslie's parents lived in Gibraltar, but they also had a villa on the Costa del Sol, in up-market Sotogrande. One weekend Leslie organised a barbeque and invited about twenty or thirty people for the weekend, on the proviso that we left the villa exactly as we had found it. Leslie and Jimmy were very friendly with a woman called Rachael who at the time worked in one of the bars that we frequented: the Three Owls. Through her they had met a couple of sisters, Julie and Denise, who had both lived in Gibraltar for many years. Julie's boyfriend, Alain, also played pool and Rachael played for the women's team. I had seen Denise before as she managed The Piazza, a bar cafeteria, which was central to the Main Street and next to the main taxi rank.

On the day of the barbeque, I arrived with Linda to find people everywhere. The villa was quite small but detached, in a great location with a beautiful garden and pool. The majority of the rooms were downstairs including a couple of bedrooms and then upstairs was the master bedroom. Leslie had allocated this room to Linda and I which meant sharing the double bed. We had been down that road some time before, but I had realised that things would never work out between us and so had tried to pull things back to a more platonic level. I knew that Linda was hoping that things would work out between us, and I was trying to be tactful and discreet as her friends thought that we were a couple. I decided to just enjoy the moment and not worry about it.

It was a brilliant evening. There is nothing better, than a balmy summer's night in fantastic company with good food and plenty of drink. The pool lights gave the garden a great atmosphere and we partied until the early hours when the lawn sprinkling system sent us all scurrying to our beds. The girls had put up tents at the back of the garden. Denise later said that she had looked forward to stretching out in the privacy of her new tent but because of the number of people who stayed the night, she shared with Julie and Alain. Apparently, she didn't sleep very well that night because someone in the house was snoring so loudly that it could be heard in the garden. That person was me!

In the early hours of the morning, cold and red eyed, Denise crept into the house, leaving Julie and Alain sprawled in her tent, and found an empty sofa in the living room to sleep on. Evidently my snoring was more bearable there. I had seen her during the evening, but it wasn't really until the next day that I finally had the chance to chat to her as we all lay by the pool, soaking up the sun and nursing hangovers.

A group of us were sharing amusing stories and anecdotes and I was recalling something that I had seen on television about a young bloke that had tried to light a fart and blew himself up in the pub. A couple of people in the group were horrified but Denise saw the funny side and started laughing. The more she laughed, the more I laughed.

After that day, I saw more and more of her as we often met up with friends on evenings out. She had obviously asked me about Linda by this time and I had explained the situation that I was in and said that I was looking for a new flat.

Finally, the day of the pool exhibition arrived. I picked Steve Davis up and took him to the venue across the road from the airport and then onto his hotel. We did have an initial hiccup when he was shocked to find that he was playing on an eight-ball pool table. He had expected a nine-ball table but it did not phase him at all. He is a professional in every sense of the word and the evening was a resounding success. I had organised a raffle and pulled out ten names of people that wanted to play. I played against him, representing Gibraltar. Finally, he did an hour of trick shots. He was brilliantly entertaining and charismatic, and the audience loved him.

After the event we went out until the early hours of the morning, and I said that I wanted to organise a similar event with Jimmy White. Steve said that he would get him to ring me to sort something out.

JIMMY WHITE, SNOOKER AND MUSIC

Denise and I became inseparable and even though we had only been together for a very short time, we talked about the future and about having a baby straight away, and I joked with Julie that Denise would be pregnant in a month. In fact, it was two months later when Denise gave me a small gift. I had no clue as to what it was or why she was giving it to me as we sat on the steps outside the back of the Piazza. I ripped off the paper to reveal a small box with a cellophane lid and inside was a tiny pair of boots, white with tiny blue bows and elasticated ankles. I stared at the box and then at her, then at the box and finally the penny dropped.
"Are you pregnant?"
"Yes, are you happy about it?"
When people talk about whirlwind romances, I know how easy it is to get swept along but we were both genuinely overjoyed with our news and even though I promised to keep it to myself for three months I started to tell everyone straight away.

I had already had a few conversations with Jimmy White by this time and had arranged for him to come over to Gibraltar to do an exhibition in February 2000. It went really well, and we got on like the proverbial house on fire. He invited me over to a tournament in the UK that he was competing in and then he came back over to Gibraltar and took part in a nine-ball international tournament which I organised and put on in St. Michael's Cave.

By now I was beginning to think about my future as a father and providing for my wife to be and our baby. Denise must have been about six months pregnant when I had the idea of staging a big concert.

There was a local band by the name of Melon Diesel who were making quite a name for themselves in Spain. They were all young enthusiastic musicians with loads of talent and ambition. I had seen them perform locally and there was talk of an interest by Sony Records. One night when I was out having a beer, I got chatting to the lead singer. I could tell straight away that, in time, the band would have problems with him as his ego was already manifesting itself. As I walked over to him, I had a small piece of paper in my hand.
"Hi mate, you are the singer with Melon Diesel, aren't you?"
"Err yeah..yeah…yeah…but I'm not doing any autographs tonight.."
That to me said it all!

"I don't want your autograph," I pointed out, "I wanna have a chat with you about doing a gig."
I have met many celebrities over the years and being egocentric is a destructive trait that can poison something potentially brilliant. He agreed to give me a couple of minutes of his time (!) and I introduced myself. He had heard of me, which is an integral part of living in a small close-knit community. It has its advantages, but it can also have its disadvantages.
I told him that I wanted to put on a big show and that I wanted Melon Diesel for the one night. He said that I had to get in touch with their agents in Spain and so the very next morning, that's exactly what I did.

I rang Melon Diesel's agent and agreed a date for the concert. I said that I was going to put them on at the old 'coach park' in Gibraltar. The Agent agreed a fee with me of £1000 for the night. They thought that the event would attract a crowd of 200-300 people. I thought that even working on those figures that if it cost me a grand to set it up and a grand for the band, I would still make a good profit, so I was happy to sign the contract.

With my usual enthusiasm and determination, I went to work straight away. I rang the Gibraltar Government Tourist Board and negotiated a deal to hire the 'coach park'. It was a massive area with a controlled access and perimeters bordered by the sea. Then I got a couple of sponsors and printed up tickets with their logos included. I visited local shops and arranged for them to be ticket outlets. One was Marble Arc, a fashion shop owned by a friend of mine and someone who Denise had known for many years. As it happened the lead singer of the band had been in his employ prior to going professional, so Raju, the owner of the business, was only too pleased to help. I think all the outlets also wanted to sponsor the event, so for £250 I printed up advertising boards.

Before I'd sold any tickets, I'd already got £3,000 which meant that I could pay for the band and the coach park without any worry. I paid £500 for poster and ticket printing, and I was still in profit. Whenever I am organising anything, I get through a vast amount of work on my own. I can delegate but I do not suffer fools and incompetence and inefficiency are just not in my vocabulary. I find it very hard to find anyone capable of working within my expected parameters and the problem that I always have is that once someone works with me, they always want to jump into the boss' shoes. I have got wiser with age and hopefully I have learned from past mistakes. Denise always moans at me that I get too friendly with whoever I get involved with in business and says that I should maintain a healthy distance. I find this difficult as every business I have been involved in has led to me socialising and there, waiting for me in the pub, is the top of the slippery slope.

This venture's green-eyed monster manifested itself in a man named Phil who I employed on a casual basis to run around doing odd jobs for me such as collecting artwork and delivering tickets. We got on well and he was eager to do as much as he could to help.

I went to the Gibraltar Chronicle, and I invited one of the reporters out to lunch. I gave him some spin about Melon Diesel and that they were on the verge of being signed by Sony and that this could well be the last gig that they played in their home country. I painted a picture of them that 'the Stones' would have been proud of and no doubt when the article headlined in the paper, the young singer's ego inflated even more! He was too immature to realise that it was a story that I had created as part of my publicity for the event. Obviously, there was truth in what I said: they were a fantastic band with loads of talent, but I painted this as their farewell and thank you gig to all their local fans, before they went off to make their fortune in the world.

Within days the forthcoming gig was the talk of the town, well the country to be more exact and tickets were flying. We had sold about six hundred tickets, but I knew that there was potential to sell a lot more and so the next day I set up a stall on Main Street, at the main taxi rank. I had printed a huge banner which I strung up between two trees. I didn't have a licence to sell the tickets on the street, but the local police authority overlooked this fact, and I was allowed to stay. The direct selling approach reaped great rewards and by the end of two days we had sold over two thousand tickets.

I commissioned a local guy, Johnny Artesani, a professional in every sense of the word, to supply the sound and lighting equipment for the concert. He had all the gear brought down from Spain, through the border into Gibraltar and I paid a local scaffolding business to construct a stage. I paid thousands for all this, safe in the knowledge that already I was well in profit.

Not wanting to get involved with the catering, I had negotiated with a local brewery and got two grand in sponsorship from Fosters, and then I sold the bar rights to someone I knew that owned a local nightclub. Part of the conditions of this agreement was that he supply the security team for the evening.

Then when everything was going so well, I had a complete nightmare for three days! I had collected ticket money from all of the venues, and I had £16,000 in cash but I couldn't get to the bank, so I took it home in a canvas bag. I hid it in one of the kitchen cupboards, out of sight, where no-one would find it. I was playing pool that night, so I grabbed something to eat with Denise and went out. I drank to excess, as usual, and staggered home in the early hours. Denise says I shouldn't drink on an empty head!

I don't even remember getting home but I inevitably did, and I had lots of stuff to sort out the next day. Bleary-eyed, I got up as soon as I could drag myself from my bed. Denise was still working full-time but it was her day off and she was up and about.
I went into the kitchen and flicked on the kettle, then blinking into the sunlight beaming in through the window, I opened the cupboard where I had put the money.
"Sweetheart!" I yelled.
Denise was in the bathroom.
"Yes?" She replied, coming into the kitchen.
"Have you moved the money?" I asked.
"No!" she replied tautly, "YOU moved the money!...You got it out last night when you came in and started counting it....and you woke me up....AGAIN!"
"Well...where did I put it?" I asked, sure that she would have the answer.
She didn't.
"I don't know where you put it!...but when you got into bed you said that you had hidden the money where no-one would ever find it."
I put the palms of my hands over my face, pressing my eyeballs with the tips of my fingers, trying to force out the memory....Now....where the hell would I have put it?!
"I know!" I said, "Well I don't know, but I remember putting it in a cupboard, sort of round a bend....I remember thinking that no-one would find it."

It was a small, one-bedroomed apartment and the kitchen was open plan with the living room. It had one small bathroom and a small hall…. one wardrobe, two cupboards in the hall. How hard could it be?

THREE DAYS SEARCHING!
I screamed at Denise; I threw the contents of cupboards into the middle of the living room floor. After hours of searching, finally in despair she sent me out and spent more hours going through every single cupboard in the place. I took the bottoms off the kitchen cabinets. We moved furniture.
THREE WHOLE DAYS SEARCHING!
I was at my wits end…I needed the money to pay expenses. We had a rubbish chute which was outside the flat in a communal area, but Denise seemed fairly confident that I had not left the apartment again after I had got into bed.
The day of the concert arrived. Denise was up and getting ready for work. I sat in the living room with my head in my hands, just staring in front of me at the empty chair opposite. The material was bright and floral with electric pinks, greens and white….hypnotised ....my eyes followed the line of the seam down the front…
"FUCKING HELL!" I screamed.
"WHAT IS IT?" Denise came rushing in, toothbrush in hand.
I dived from the sofa and grabbed the canvas bag which was tucked under the chair opposite.
Laughing hysterically with relief, I opened the bag and looked inside…stacks of notes. I blew out a sigh.
"Well, that is some kind of cupboard!" Denise fumed, "..round a bend, where no-one can find it!"
"The bag must have slid with the chair when I moved it to look." I apologised.
"You said that you put it in a cupboard! Three days we've been looking for that and all the time it was under the chair!"
She went to work. She wasn't happy because at one point I had even accused her of taking it!

I walked with Denise and some friends down to the venue. Now I was going to enjoy the night. The atmosphere was electric and with the sea behind and the Rock of Gibraltar as a stage backdrop, things couldn't have been better. The stage and lighting were fantastic. The sound system was phenomenal, and the local supporting bands all did themselves proud. Denise knew a couple of great musicians, Giles Ramirez and Stephen McLaren. . They were popular on the local music scene, and they put on an amazing performance, whipping the crowd up into a frenzy of anticipation for the main band.

I had seen a van arrive with blacked out windows and I knew that these young local lads were actually starting to believe that they could take the world by storm. My opinion of them was sinking rapidly as earlier in the day I had been contacted by their Agent with a 'rider' listing all sorts of drinks, different sized towels, ice, food, etc that they would be requiring in their dressing room later. My suspicions that they had completely lost the plot were confirmed when I was summoned to the dressing room by their manager and told that Melon Diesel would not be going on stage unless I gave them ten thousand pounds!! This was nine thousand more than our contract! Refusing to be held to ransom, I said that I would wait until after the supporting bands had finished and then I would go onstage with my contract and tell the audience that they were refusing to honour their side, that they were prepared to disappoint all their fans because they were demanding more money.

I went back to Denise and the others and said that I was having a few problems, but I did not let on the extent of the pressure that I was being put under. I watched as Melon Diesel got back into their van and drove out of the venue. I was so tempted to just leave with the cash that I had, and I played out in my mind the sequence of events that could follow. I would send my copy of the contract to the Gibraltar Chronicle and expose them for the scheming manipulative chancers that they were…..or…..
My mobile rang.
It was Dillon the lead singer.
"George, we are about to go back up to Madrid. You have to make your mind up, are we playing or not?"
I told them to get back to the venue in five minutes and I would talk to them.
As soon as they arrived, I got one of my friends to let down the tyres on the van, so a swift departure was out of the question, unless they fancied running through a crowd of angry ticketholders!
I told them that they were a bunch of cunts and that the manager was a bitch, and then I handed over £10,000 in cash and they went on stage to a rapturous welcome from an oblivious audience.

I went back to join Denise. The concert was brilliant and will probably go down in Gibraltar history. Afterwards we walked along to a nightclub, Cool Blues, that was owned by some of Denise's friends. We stood at the bar and after one drink I looked at her, smiled and asked,
"Shall we go home? I could just eat egg and chips."

That's exactly what we did. We left everyone partying late into the early hours of the morning. We walked back to the flat and on the way, I told Denise what had gone on with the band.

Melon Diesel did go on tour, but it wasn't long before they were dropped by Sony and as far as I know they have been absorbed back into normality. It is a shame because they had great talent and even greater potential.

After that, I put on a couple of darts exhibitions, bringing over Eric Bristow and Chris Mason and I organised after-dinner speakers, putting on events at the local casino with Rodney Marsh and Tommy Docherty, the latter of whom visited Denise in hospital a couple of days after our son was born.

THE HAPPIEST DAY OF MY LIFE

The arrival of our little man into the world will be a day that I will never forget, and it is the happiest day of my life. A week earlier, Denise had been taken into hospital but was then sent home again and asked to return in a week's time if nothing had happened. She was admitted and induced the following Saturday and then on the Sunday at about ten o'clock I got a call from one of the nurses asking me to go to the hospital, that Denise was fine, but would like some help with a crossword!

When I got there, she was in the labour room! I thought that I was useless throughout the labour, taking the gas and air and eating any food that was brought in for Denise, but she said that I was great and that it was laughing at me that got her through the seventeen hours.

On Monday at 2pm a decision was made for an emergency caesarean operation to be carried out. We were both exhausted and we cried together when we were told that I would not be able to go into the theatre. Denise was given an epidural so that she could stay awake, and I stood outside in the corridor, still crying. I phoned Alain, Julie's boyfriend, and sobbed down the phone prompting him to leave work and rush to my side, closely followed by Julie and Denise's very close friend, Juliet. Finally, after what seemed like an eternity, Maria, our midwife, opened the door carrying a blue bundle.
"Here he is.... your son." she said holding him out to me.
I could hardly see him through the tears. He was the most perfect beautiful thing that I had ever seen. Denise said that as soon as he was born Maria wrapped him up and put him next to her face. She put her fingers on his cheek and kissed him and said, "There you are!" And then she looked at Maria and said,
"Take him to his daddy."
Denise was more aware than anyone about my concerns for our baby after what had happened to Anna, and she had told Maria about it when I wasn't around.
So, Lewis George Bamby came into the world, weighing a healthy 8lb 6oz.

Denise and I bought a flat in the town centre. She had given up work to look after the baby and life for her changed overnight. I still went out drinking whenever I wanted to, often staying out all night or I would bring friends back and we would sit on the patio chatting and laughing

and drinking even more. One morning she got up in the early hours with Lewis and stamped into the bedroom,
"George, have you been sick on the baby!?"
In actual fact, in a drunken stupor I had made a sandwich of some ratatouille that she had put in the fridge and as I was coo-cooing over him before going to bed, I had dribbled it onto his blanket, dropping chunks of tomato and aubergine into the cot.
"What if he had choked on something!?" she was irate and understandably so.
I didn't change. I think that is probably when her resentment of me started.

Often when I would get home drunk, in the early hours, I would ring my Auntie Dot or my Auntie Shirley. Having Lewis and seeing how Denise was with him made me think more and more about my own childhood and like a dark fog it settled over my life. For many years before that, I used to get my stepfather's phone number and would ring him and tell him that he was complete wanker. Denise heard me on the phone asking my cousin David for the number and wanted to know what I wanted it for. I told her that I wanted to ring him up and remind him what a useless sack of shit he is. Ever the philosopher, she insisted that unless I was getting something positive out of doing that then it was a pointless thing to do. I knew what she meant but I hated to think that he was just getting on with his life whilst I had been robbed of my childhood and was left with the burdening weight of the injustice that I felt.

A couple of days later Denise heard me on the phone to an estate agent talking about a house that was for sale in Manchester.
"Now, what are you doing?!" she knew that I was up to something.
"Our Kelly is selling her house and I'm going to get a phone number for her"
She stood and listened whilst I blagged the number out of the unsuspecting estate agent. Then I rang Kelly's number pretending to be from the estate agents and she unwittingly gave me the number for our mother and her father.
"If you are going to ring, then at least try and have a conversation. Don't just ring up and start swearing at him" Denise pleaded.
"He's a fat fucker and he can fuck off" I said, but I thought about what she was saying to me, and it made sense, well sort of.

The number burnt a hole in my pocket. I took it out and looked at it. I put it on the desk, on the coffee table, under a lamp, back on the desk. As I slept, I imagined it glowing in the dark of the living room.
Sweating and screaming, I woke in the night, imagining the figure of my stepdad bearing down upon me, fists clenched, teeth clamped together as he came to kill me in my bed.

A couple of days later, I sat at my desk at home, staring at the piece of paper with their number scrawled on it in black ink. I screwed up the paper and threw it to the back of the desk and made a couple of phone calls. I was accustomed to working with my phone in 'speaker' mode. Denise found it stressful listening to me as I can be an aggressive negotiator, if need be, and I was under a lot of pressure and very irritable.
"That's it….I'm ringing!" I said uncurling the crumpled paper.
Denise came to my side.
"Just try not to shout and swear" she urged "I don't know…talk to him, it might help you to move on with your life."
"I have fucking moved on!" I was sure that I had but then why was I sitting at my desk now, phone in hand and why was I still having nightmares about him.
"If you'd moved on you wouldn't still be ringing him up and swearing at him." Denise said, "Maybe if you talk to him, you can really start to put it all behind you. Just don't ring up and start swearing, that's not getting anywhere, that doesn't do you any good."

"Hello"
"Hello"
"Who's that?"
It was my mother at the other end of the line.
"It's George…don't you even recognise your own son's voice?"
"Fuck off!" she slammed the phone down.

I rang again.
"Hello George, what do you want?"
It was him. My flesh went cold, and my heart thumped against the inside of my chest. Even now, like a trained Pavlovian dog, his voice instilled fear.
Denise was at my side; she could hear him on the speaker phone. She nodded in encouragement for me to speak to him. I don't even remember what I said at first, I think that I told him about Lewis and

maybe Denise. She busied herself behind me trying to keep out of the way, but she said that she was listening and was happy that so far, I hadn't lost it and started swearing at him. I remember that he kept asking me what I wanted and so I said that I wanted some answers. I asked him,
"Why did you do all of those things to me? Why did you make me eat dog food? Why did you shoot at me with an air rifle? "
"George.." he said, "we were just having a laugh."
"A laugh?!.....It wasn't a fucking laugh!…I was a boy."
He said something about him being young at the time and asked me again what I wanted. I said that he had never even said sorry for treating me the way he did, and he actually said that he was sorry and asked me to get on with my life.
Suddenly his mood changed.
"You're taping this." he said. It was a statement, not a question.
"No, I'm not."
"I can hear the tape recorder….What's that noise then?"
I looked around the room. We had a small fan heater on. It was one of those thermostatically controlled units, a small rectangular box with three heat setting buttons on the top. Now I wonder if it had switched on in the background whilst we were talking. I was not even aware of it.
"It's a fan heater." I assured him.
He didn't want to talk anymore.
"Just get on with your life George"
That was it.
Denise was back at my side.
"I can't believe that he said that" she was shaking her head and had tears in her eyes.
"What?"
"I can't believe that he said that they were just having a laugh."
When I thought about it, I realised what a shocking statement it was.

The next day Denise told Julie and Juliet and anyone else that would listen what he had said. She asked me if I could imagine treating Lewis like that for a laugh. She thought it incredulous that he should think that an acceptable excuse for my mistreatment.
"They had a laugh" she said "and you suffered the consequences and even though you think you have put it behind you, it does impact on your life. How do you feel now? Hopefully now that he has apologised you might be able to start putting it behind you."

Immediately after the phone call I felt great but the day after I felt angry again.
"Do you know what?" I asked Denise, prompting her to ask what my next plan of attack was.
"What?"
"I'm going to take that bastard to court. I'm going to take out a civil case against him and I am going……"
"Can't you just put it behind you now? You've got your own family to worry about." Denise thought that I might get on with things after the call. Little did she know that call was only the beginning.

"I'm going to start writing everything down…and try to get it all in some sort of order…..D'you know how many fucking schools I went to?.. and the kids homes, foster parents…I'll write down everything..and all about what that bastard did…and then I'm going to take him to court."
I lay down on the sofa recalling the telephone conversation and then I jumped up,
"Do you know what?" I asked Denise
"What?"
"I should have fucking taped it…that phone conversation."
That day I started making notes about all the incidents that I could remember.

Life continued as before and one day as I was staggering home mid-morning, still drunk from the night before, I saw Denise pushing Lewis in the pram. She crossed over the road to avoid me and when I got home, I cried because I was so disgusted with myself. I went to a local AA meeting wondering if I was an alcoholic. It wasn't that I would drink in the day, but if I went out in the evening I would drink and drink and drink and when the bars closed, I would go to anyone's house that was happy to carry on the party.

I stopped drinking completely for a while but then eventually I started again although not to the same extent. For the next couple of years, I tried to get a decent business up and running that would support our family. I set up a building company, but things seemed to go from bad to worse and I fell out with the guy that I had taken on as a partner. I always found the money for the mortgage, but bills were going unpaid, and debts were mounting. This put more strain on my relationship with Denise. She started working part time at the bar cafeteria that she used to manage, putting Lewis into a nursery for three mornings a week. As things worsened, I knew that drastic action was needed.

We left Gibraltar, going to Ireland for a few months where Denise's brother lived, and then to England. I left Denise to pack up the flat, sort out the rental and ship all our things over whilst I went ahead to get things ready for her and Lewis's arrival. She says that she got the short straw in the deal. She had someone hammering on the door on a few occasions, someone that I owed money to. She didn't answer but hid in the flat with Lewis, trying to keep him quiet so the man at the door didn't realise that she was inside. She was still working and taking care of Lewis. I didn't realise quite what a wrench it was for her to leave. She had lived there for over twenty years and in fact she says that she did contemplate staying there without me. When leaving day came, she got the flight with a load of luggage, a toddler and a suitcase full of regrets.

JIMMY WHITE AND GOING SNOOKER LOOPY

I had kept in touch with Jimmy White during this time and went to see him quite often. I organised some exhibitions with him, up and down the country and I organised a couple of tournaments overseas. I worked as an agent taking commission from any events that I booked him to attend and on a personal level we became great friends. I stayed at his house, and we went out and played snooker at his local club.

On one such visit I got far more than I bargained for. We were going over to Switzerland to do an exhibition and I had arranged to stay over at Jimmy's house. A friend of his picked me up from the airport. I had met him before, so we easily got into a conversation during the trip, and he told me that he had split up with his wife and that there had been some sort of altercation with her new boyfriend. I think it may have been over the dog, but I can't remember the details. She had an injunction out against him and allegedly he was being denied contact with his kids. He said that he had sent mobile phones to his daughters, with his number programmed in so they could contact him, but somewhere along the line the police had got involved.

We arrived at Jimmy's house, had something to eat, then the three of us played pool and drank our way into the evening. At about 11pm Jimmy went off to bed and Mark and I stayed up drinking bottles of Bud and talking until about half one. Jimmy had a fruit machine which kept us entertained for a few hours.

At about half six in the morning, my mind leapt from unconsciousness to adrenaline-fuelled alertness as I opened my eyes to find four men in suits standing at the side of the bed. The rush of blood to my head and the beat of my heart must have been almost audible in the room. I sat bolt upright and then was virtually dragged, naked, from beneath the sheets.

"You are coming with us; you are under arrest." One of the suits was speaking.

There was total confusion on my part. I was only just realising where I was. I don't think that I could even manage to speak.

I heard something like, "...intimidating a witness...."

Still confused, I looked from face to face, suit to suit.

Handcuffs!

Then I found my voice.

"What the fuck is going on?"

I looked again at the faces, then in the background by the door, I saw the face of Jimmy White, in his boxer shorts, scratching his head. He was laughing.
"Jimmy, what the fuck is going on?" I asked.
Jimmy smiled and in his smooth Cockney drawl he said, "Er…sorry boys, you've got the wrong bedroom…er…Mark is in the bedroom over there."
He pointed to the door opposite.
"What's your name?" one of the men in black asked.
"George Bamby! What the fuck is your name? Cos I'm going to get yer fucking done for this!"
They uncuffed me, apologising as they did so and then went off to arrest Mark who was still sleeping soundly in the room across the corridor. Jimmy thought the whole episode was hilarious and in fact gave it a mention in his autobiography!

I carried on working with Jimmy and by now I had bought a house with Denise, in Stoke-on-Trent. I worked away a lot and this gave me the perfect excuse to conceal the affairs I was having. I sometimes had a conscience, but I convinced myself that what Denise didn't know wouldn't hurt her. The more I got away with it, the more women I got involved with. I lied and lied until it became second nature, and I did it without any guilt. Denise trusted me, so she never questioned my behaviour but things between us deteriorated.

At the World Championships in Sheffield, Jimmy introduced me to a young Australian player, Quinten Hann. I think that he was about number 11 in the world rankings at the time, and I spoke to him about becoming his Manager. I knew everything about the game of snooker, I had fantastic contacts and before the day was over the contract was in the bag.

A few months later, Quinten was playing against a guy called Andy Hicks in the World Championships which was being broadcast by the BBC. Quinten needed to win the match to stay in the top sixteen ranked players. For anyone that doesn't know about snooker, any player that falls below the sixteenth place, has to play in all of the preliminaries to get into any tournaments. Only the top 16 ranked players are guaranteed places.

Quinten was goading Andy Hicks as they played. The two of them had a bit of prior history as Quinten always wound-up Andy whenever they played against each other. This day was no exception. Every opportunity he got to make a sly comment, Quinten whispered insults and abuse at his opponent. The outcome of the match was that Andy won and he strode over to shake Quinten's hand. He refused and hurled further abuse. Andy didn't retaliate but he asked Quinten what he had just said. The Australian lifted the butt of his cue in a mock assault, as if he was about to strike Andy about the head with it. Quinten swore again and the referee had to intervene. This, I believe, was the first time ever in the history of world snooker that a referee has had to get involved to separate two players.

As they left the arena, Andy Dillon, from the Press Office approached me and asked me what had gone on and said that they were organising a press conference. I said that I would speak to Quinten and then we would talk to them in a few minutes.

The World Snooker Championships is the last event in the snooker calendar, leaving the players with a three-month break before the start of the next season. I took Quinten to one side and said that I had a brilliant idea of how to take advantage of what had happened. Quinten was still breathing fire and spitting profanities at that stage and threatening to make his verbal assault physical.
"How do you fancy getting in the ring and having a proper boxing match with him?"
"Fucking yeah! Too fucking right! Great idea mate. Sort it out!" He left me with no uncertainty that he was whole-heartedly behind the idea.

I sent Quinten back to the hotel and I went into the press conference representing him as his manager. I said that Quinten was particularly fiery and that he had taken a disliking to a number of the English players, one of whom was Andy Hicks. I then went on to name a few others, one of whom I hoped would be up to participating in a boxing event. Mark King is a friend of mine and it was him who rose to the occasion. Andy Hicks had already declined the offer of getting into a fight and when I spoke to Mark and offered him a purse of £10,000 if he would get into the ring, it was motivation enough. Mark came into the press conference and defended the honour of his buddy Andy Hicks by offering to be his champion in battle. I couldn't have scripted it better myself.

That night the story was covered by all the major television networks and the tabloids had a field day the following morning. It was excellent spin, and it created a wave of excitement amongst the snooker fraternity and major controversy amongst the officials. Some saw it as much needed publicity for the sport, which was losing sponsorship deals hand over fist, whilst others thought that it was bringing the sport into disrepute.

The next day I hired a venue, the York Hall in Bethnal Green, London, and I contacted Keith Waters, Chairman of the Amateur Boxing Association. After completing all thc rclcvant paperwork and medicals and by meeting the required criteria with the regard to age and health, Mark King and Quinten Hann were registered as amateur boxers and were able to compete in an officially sanctioned bout. I planned to have them as top of the bill and then on the 'undercard' I arranged for the Repton and Dagenham Boxing Clubs, both in London, to compete in seven further bouts.

As soon as I had secured the venue, the date, and the licences, I organised a press conference where I gave details of our forthcoming POT WHACK event. The majority of the press were from weekly newspapers and magazines and so, as they were all preparing to leave, I asked Darren Lewis from the Mirror and Andy Dillon from the Sun to stay behind and then I said that we would do the press conference again. There were a few confused faces until I explained that I wanted to stage a mock bust-up, mid interview, which would create a great story for the dailies and superb publicity for us. My only stipulation was that on the bottom of the editorials I asked that they include the website address for the ticket sales. Stan James, the bookmakers, well **stanjames.com** to be exact, sponsored the fight and set up a link from their website to purchase tickets.

The next morning, I got the two papers and there were double page spreads in each. At half eleven I logged onto the website to check how the ticket sales were going. We had a seating plan for 1356 people which filled the venue to capacity. We had sold out.

Denise set up an office at home and liaised with Stan James in Gibraltar. She organised the seating plan and despatched all the tickets over the next week, often working into the early hours of the morning. It was great to be able to offload that responsibility and it gave me time to work on other things. I got a further sponsorship deal from EA Sports and arranged for Nuts magazine to supply a couple of their models to be inter-round 'card girls'. My mobile rang non-stop until the day of the fight. Denise sorted out all the press passes and she and her friend, Paula, went to the venue on the night and manned a desk on the door where they organised the VIP tickets and the Press.

On the evening of the big event, the sons of the Sultan of Brunei turned up, so we had to accommodate them as additional guests. I did get a cash windfall from doing so though, so it was worth the inconvenience, and they left before the main fight anyway. We had many celebrity faces in the crowd including Keith Allen, someone who I would later work with. The atmosphere was charged and when Ronnie O'Sullivan came into Quinten's dressing room, it was great to have him on our side. Quinten was very much the underdog, and his supporters were thin on the ground compared to the overwhelming support for London boy, Mark King.

The whole building vibrated to its core as the boxers came out into their corners. The capacity audience chanted and cheered themselves into a testosterone-fuelled frenzy. Ronnie and I walked out in front of Quinten, holding the belt over our heads and soaking up the waves of adrenaline. The sounds of the Australian band 'Men at Work' singing 'Down Under' heralded Quinten's arrival in the blue corner. It was a fantastic experience.

It was a great fight. I am sure that technically the Amateur Boxing Association could pick holes in the performance but both boxers had trained hard, and they put everything into it. It was fantastic entertainment for every second of the three two-minute rounds. Quinten was given the victory on points but both fighters were brilliant as far as I was concerned. Neither of them had boxed before, they had been trained at their local boxing clubs in a very short time and they did themselves proud. Mark King was a good mate, so I was not happy to see him with a couple of nasty cuts where Quinten had caught him. I think that many people had expected Mark to win but Quinten had the determination of a demented dingo.

After the fight, we all went onto a nightclub and celebrated into the early hours. My night was made even better by meeting Denzel Washington in a nightclub. The whole evening was amazing from my point of view.

Denise's brother and his girlfriend were at the fight with Denise and Paula and an old friend of theirs from Gibraltar had arrived. I didn't invite them to join us in the celebrations and they all went back to their hotel, which suited me as I had my current girlfriend in the crowd. I was living an exciting life and Denise was not part of it.

I stayed involved with snooker for some time and I signed a few more players including another Australian, Neil Robertson and an up-and-coming lad from Coventry by the name of Mark Selby. I recognised Mark for the brilliant player that he was to become and in fact he was in the final of the World Championships in 2007. I did more exhibitions with Jimmy White, John Virgo, Alex Higgins, Ronnie O'Sullivan, Matthew Stephens, Mark King, Ali Carter, Quinten Hann and Mark Selby.

A MOVE TO DEVON

Early in 2004, Denise and I decided to relocate to Devon. She had made no friends in Stoke-on-Trent and even though she had family in the area she was becoming increasingly unsettled. One day as I passed an estate agent's window, I saw a similar property to ours for sale at a much higher price than we had paid six months earlier. Without consulting Denise, I arranged for the estate agent to come in and have a look at our property. She soon came around to the idea of moving and before long we had made an offer on a property in Devon. That house purchase fell through and when I was working away and Denise found another house that she liked, I just told her to put an offer in. Luckily, I loved it as soon as I walked in and saw a wall almost entirely of glass with a balcony and spectacular views over the woods.

By the time we moved in though, which was in August, I had made quite a few business commitments in Manchester and before I could lay down roots in our new home, I found myself staying away more and more. By November, unbeknown to Denise, I was living with Karen, a woman that I had met in Hale, Cheshire. It was complicated as she had a long-term partner who was working away at the time. The first few months of any relationship are lust-fuelled and neither of us cared about the hurt that we would cause. We were inseparable and I thought, as I did when I met Denise, that this time I had found my soul mate. It was an exciting time: we had a fantastic social life, something that I didn't have with Denise. I made more celebrity friends and life was one long party.
A few weeks before Christmas, Karen's partner was due back which meant that I had to move out of the house. I went back to Devon, to Denise and Lewis, who were happy to have me at home for a while. Although I was happy to see my son, I resented Denise and longed to be back with Karen and my life in Cheshire.

I was an emotional wreck and I wondered if I would ever get my life on track. One day as I sat in the office at home, talking to Denise, I said that I was going to set up a website to raise money to take my mother and stepdad to court. She did not like the idea, but she has always supported me in everything that I have done. That day I registered the domain name and before the day was over, I had the site up and running.

Whilst we were in Stoke, I had started writing down all my memories of incidents that had happened in my childhood and so I put all the bits together on the site. Denise was still not happy with the concept of what

I wanted to do, asking people for money and so out of the blue she asked,
"Why don't you report them to the police?"
"Don't be stupid." I said, "What are the police going to do now, after all these years?"
"Well, I think that if you report it, they would have to investigate."
She had a cousin who was an ex-police officer, so we decided to ring him but when he wasn't in we left it there, but the seed had been planted. The next day I rang the police in Manchester who gave me the number for the Child Protection Unit. When I made that call, little did I know that I was about to embark on an incredible journey.

By the New Year I was back in Cheshire with Karen, Denise still happy in her ignorance had been decorating our bedroom. I went in to meet with Graham Jones from the Manchester Child Protection Unit and I spent days making my statement. For the first time, someone in authority listened to what I had to say, and I cried the tears of a small boy. I relived the days of my childhood, opening old wounds and taking my first tentative steps towards recovery and closure.

After three days giving statements, I was physically and mentally exhausted, wondering if I was doing the right thing but at the same time driven by the possibility that I might actually be able to face my tormentors in a court of law. Graham explained that it was going to be a long and difficult road that we would be walking but that we would be doing it together. He said from the very beginning that to get a conviction without material evidence was going to be very difficult, but he promised me that I would have my day in court. Graham had worked for many years with children of all ages in all sorts of abusive situations, but I think that even though my case was unique, he knew that like all the other children I needed closure and I needed to know that the people that had abused me were to be made accountable for their actions. That day when I met Graham, I made a friend for life, and I will be eternally in his debt. He renewed my faith in humanity. He was prepared to stick out his neck and knowing that he was fighting against the odds, he took my case on.

Now I had to be patient and let the cogs of the judicial system turn in their own time. There were months of research to be done before we reached the point where my mother and stepfather would be arrested. I dreamt about it; I pictured them being led away to a waiting car, my mother in handcuffs, shouting, my stepfather yelling that I was a liar, that I had always been a liar; I had nightmares that my stepdad would come into my room at night to kill me. One night I was at home with Denise, who was still oblivious to the double life that I was leading, and I woke up sweating and screaming. She was terrified, woken by me shouting that he was in the room, and she said that I was screaming like I was being murdered. Both of us slept badly that night, each listening to the other breathing and watching the shadows dancing on the wall. It was only one of many nightmares that I have had over the years, each one the same and for all my bravado that I had put the past behind me, I knew that somewhere, in a dark recess, it still haunted me. I couldn't change the past but maybe I could find a way forward to better future.

THE IRISH FIGHT

Quinten loved boxing. He had enjoyed the training and was quite fit by that time. As he still had a couple of snooker-free months, he was enthusiastic when I suggested a second fight. I had a few contacts in Ireland, so I rang a guy that I knew from the Daily Star, the Irish issue, and arranged to meet him in Jurys Hotel in Dublin.

Quinten and I flew over the next day, but I despatched my prodigy to get breakfast whilst I had the first meeting. The journalist was expecting a great story and so I gave him one. I said that Quinten had said that all the Gaelic footballers in Ireland were effeminate shithouses and that even though they looked tough he reckoned that he could kick the shit out of any of them. It was a slight exaggeration on my part, but I had his interest. I then went on to say that Quinten was so confident in his own superior prowess over them, that he was prepared to offer a purse of 10,000 euros to anyone that would get into the boxing ring with him

The next day, the front page of the Irish Daily Star headlined with the story. There were photographs of Quinten and editorial about what I alleged he had said. The gauntlet had been well and truly thrown down. The following day the Daily Star was inundated with calls, not only from footballers, the whole Irish community was up in arms and there were offers to take up the challenge from every pub in Dublin!

Then a phone call came through from the head of the Gaelic Football Association: They had taken the bait.... game on! The caller said that he had a guy named Johnny McGee that would fight Quinten. He played for the 'Dubs', which was the Dublin main football team. We couldn't have caught a better fish. Demographically I knew we would be onto a winner with the ticket sales. I asked him to fax a picture through so that we could have a look at him, and he looked like a big guy! Quinten didn't hesitate, he said that he would take him on.

The next day the newspapers were full of the Johnny McGee versus Quinten Hann fight. They wanted to know who these two mouthy guys were, going over to their country, one from Australia, and one from New Zealand (that would be me then!).

I contacted the Irish Boxing Association and got the licences for both boxers. Then I hired the National Stadium which had a capacity of 2,500 people. Tickets went on sale for 40 euros each and I organised a press conference to be held at Drimnheh (pronounced Drimnar) Boxing

Club. We had TV3 there, RTE 1, all the radio stations and newspapers. I had prepped Johnny McGee up beforehand so that he knew what to expect: I said that I would retaliate strongly to something that he would say, and I would throw a glass of water over him. Johnny said that was fine but not to throw too much water as he had to go back to work and that he couldn't go back soaking. Hilarious!

The press conference started, and I introduced myself and Quinten and as a formality, for he was well-known in Ireland, Johnny McGee. I said that Quinten and Johnny were going to get in the ring and prove whether Ozzie rules footballers were harder than Gaelic footballers. Someone asked me what I thought, being Quinten's manager, who did I **want** to win and then he asked me, who did I **think** would win. When I said that I thought Quinten would win, he asked why I was so confident. Cockily, I said that they should look at Johnny McGee, that he was a fat bastard and that he looked like a Teletubby. Johnny McGee rose to the occasion and said that I had a big mouth. I told him to shut up and called him a prick. He looked at me in a strange way, anticipating what was to come next and so I said, "I'll knock you out me-self!"
I reached out to get the glass of water that was in front of me, but Quinten had drunk it, so I picked up the next best thing, a full jug! I threw it in Johnny's face and jumped out of my chair. All our bodyguards jumped into the affray and the table went over.

Brilliant publicity! The next day every newspaper carried the story with photographs. On TV, it led the news stories which was absolutely ridiculous. The tickets sales flew. The next day, we got a call inviting us to go on Good Morning TV which we did. I was also interviewed on the Joe Duffy show on the radio which was an hour-long show in which people can ring in and usually guests were only on for a short time. Apparently, that was the first time that anyone had stayed on for the whole hour. I was deliberately obnoxious, winding up the callers, all the time aware that it was free publicity for the event. One woman rang in, and she said,
"D'ya know George, you sound like a really horrible man, ya come over here and ya say all these tings about the Irish and I hope this Johnny McGee beats Quinten up"
I said, "He's not going to beat Quinten up."
"How can you be so sure?" she was eager to know.
I said, "I can be sure…you obviously don't know anything about boxing" and I went on,"Why don't you go back in the kitchen and make

a cup of tea, come back in the front room and sit down and put yer feet up and carry on with yer knitting? You are talking about something that you have no idea about. Thanks a lot, next caller please"
I must have had the Irish listeners screaming at their radios, and if any of them are reading this I would say…things are not always what they seem. The media has the power to manipulate, to build up and to strike down. We are all at their mercy as long as people buy newspapers.
The callers were endless and then suddenly Joe Duffy said,
"I have someone on the line here, George, that wants to have a chat with you. He's the former heavyweight champion, Steve Collins."
I knew who he was, he had fought people like Nigel Benn and Chris Eubanks. His call came through and he said,
"George, ya know I think you've got a big mouth coming over here…."
"Can I just stop you for a minute?" I interrupted "What did you say your name was?"
He said, "It's Steve Collins!"
"Steve Collins?" I repeated "I've never heard of you mate, what do you do?"
"I'm the former Irish heavyweight champion…" he said indignantly
"Listen mate," I said, glad that we were linked only over the air waves, "I've been involved in boxing for years and I've never heard of ya. I'm sure if you were any good, I would have heard of you."
I deliberately wound him up, but I knew that the next day it would be the talk of the town, if not the country.

Quinten and I were not popular visitors. A couple of days before the fight we came out of the hotel and walked along the street to buy some newspapers and magazines and about eight burly blokes started shouting abuse.
"There's those pair o' cunts!" and they chased us along the road.
After that I had to employ security to look after us until the fight was over. The whole of Ireland wanted to kill us, and we had to be on our guard 24/7.
I have some great friends who are Irish, the Irish people are wonderful, their country is beautiful, but obviously my hype was believable, and I was public enemy number ONE.

The National Stadium was three-quarters full for the fight. It wasn't as good as I had hoped it would be as I wanted it to be bursting at the seams. Still, it was a great night and we made quite a bit of money but considering our personal safety, after the fight we left the dressing room, got into the back of a van and were driven straight to the ferry port. On the ferry, we drank ourselves into oblivion, relieved to be out of the country alive. In Holyhead, we checked into a hotel, where we both got a well-deserved sleep and woke up to work out how much money we had made.

QUINTEN'S DEMISE

I had signed Quinten for a twelve-month contract and during that time he had been arrested on charges of a sexual assault and assault causing actual bodily harm. This was the second time that this had happened: the previous time he had been acquitted of a rape charge. I got a phone call from the Sun newspaper in the early hours of the morning, asking me for a comment and they told me that he had been arrested. I stated that I couldn't possibly comment until I had spoken to Quinten. Straightaway, I drove to London where I waited for him at the police station and picked him up when he was bailed at about four o'clock in the afternoon. The press was there so I told Quinten that he should release one statement to the papers. He did that saying that the allegations were unfounded and that he was glad that the police were involved so that he could clear his name, that it was a woman trying to get money out of him.

As we drove away, I asked Quinten what had happened. He said that he and a couple of mates had picked up three girls in China Whites nightclub and gone back to his flat. His apartment was big with contemporary furnishings, and I think that the fact that he had a Ferrari outside may have suggested that he had money. He said that she had been online and looked him up and that when she went to leave, she tried to take his keys with her. Allegedly, according to Quinten, he had grabbed her bag and she ended up on the floor as she had been drinking. The poor woman had smashed teeth! He said that she had hit the wall opposite…

Over the next few months, I kept overhearing conflicting snippets of events and it was enough for me to doubt the integrity of the man that I had agreed to manage. On top of that were a couple more incidents and I began to wonder if Quinten was actually the person that he portrayed. Outwardly he was good-looking and successful, but I was convinced that he had a dangerous, ugly streak and that after a drink he lost his self-control. By this time, he owed me about nine thousand pounds' commission from his prize money, but he refused to pay me, preferring to spend my money maintaining his playboy lifestyle.

After numerous reasonable requests, I finally gave him an ultimatum: either he paid me, or I would make sure that he would never pick up a snooker cue again.
"Are you threatening me?" he asked.
"No, I'm not threatening you." I said, "I'm not going to have someone break your arms or your legs or anything, there are other ways of doing things."
We ended up having a huge row and he told me to fuck off and swore that I would never get any money off him.

I was managing a few other young players at the time and at the snooker events Quinten started bad-mouthing me, saying that I had ripped him off with the boxing, which was a complete lie. I had signed another young Australian, by the name of Neil Robertson and Quinten was convincing enough to make him want to cancel his contract with me. At the same time, I was made aware of an incident in Ireland that had caused ructions in the area we stayed. It involved Quinten and another girl but for legal reasons, as I was not witness to the incident, and to protect the girl involved I will not go into details here. I was disgusted with him, and it was enough to make me want to knock him of his pedestal. I silently vowed to expose Quinten for the person that he was. To Quinten, I said that he was messing with the wrong person. He said that I would have to get up early to get one over on him. The next day I was up with the larks planning his downfall. My contacts at the Sun newspaper had already become interested in the complaints that had been brought against him.

Quinten had always spouted off to me that first and foremost he was a businessman, that he hated snooker and that all he cared about was money. At the next tournament, I approached Quinten and said that we should put our arguments behind us because an opportunity had presented itself where he could get a load of money. I said that a couple of friends of mine from Gibraltar had been working for a big betting company, but they had left and one of them had just inherited £200,000. I said that he wanted to bet a load of money on a fixed snooker result. He was in….immediately! He apologised for trying to shaft me and said that we could have a fresh start, and both get a load of money.

A few days later, I sat down with a reporter and an undercover investigator from the Sun newspaper, and we worked out our plan of attack. Not many weeks later Quinten was due to play in the Qualifiers at Pontins, Prestatyn. Anyone that is not in the top sixteen players must compete for a place in the World Championships. I rang up Pontins and I reserved room 147 which being the highest break in snooker was appropriate for the place where Quinten would hit the lowest point in his career.

Inside the room, the journalists and myself wired the television up with a hidden camera and concealed further cameras around the room. The two guys from the Sun were also 'wired up' and we had a second apartment across the path where a photographer was strategically placed with the door open. The men had hired a fire red Ferrari from Birmingham which gave credibility to the story, and I knew that once Quinten saw that, he would be sucked in. At the culmination of his qualifying match, I pulled Quinten to one side.
"The boys are here." I said, nodding to the exit.
We went down to room 147 and the guys came out to meet us.
"Hi George, how are you doing?" asked the investigator.
"Brian, this is Quinten." I said, stepping to one side.
As they shook hands, Quinten still in his white shirt and waistcoat, the camera shutter opposite captured everything. We went into the room, and I introduced them all formally and then I said that I was leaving them to talk. I said to Quinten that if he needed me, I would be sitting outside in the car. After about forty-five minutes, Quinten emerged.
"George," he said, bending down to the car window, "Are these guys Kosher?"
"Of course, they are fucking Kosher!" I said.

Minutes later, we both went back into the room and Quinten said that he was playing Ken Doherty in the China Open the following month and he said that he would lose the match 5 – 3. I asked Quinten how he could guarantee losing 5 to 3 if they were having loads of money on it. I said surely if you are going to lose you would have to lose five to nil. He said that he could not possibly lose five to nil, that he would look stupid. I asked him what would happen then if he had a really bad day, and he did get beaten five to nil and Brian and Gary had bet on him losing five to three. He then suggested making it five to two. I said that the only score that he could possibly guarantee would be five to nil and having thought about it, Quinten agreed. I said that I was going to leave them

again, that I didn't want to be involved in what they were sorting out. After I left, on the tapes I heard him say that he didn't want me involved in it and that the money would be for him alone. There was five grand in cash on the table which Brian said was a down payment.
"Nice one!"
Quinten picked up the money and put it in his pocket.
He went back to the competition hall, and I went in to have a chat with the guys from the Sun. They had everything on tape, and they had photographs, but they had been onto the newsdesk and a decision had been made to sit on the story until they knew the outcome of Quinten's pending sexual assault charge.

About four or five weeks later, Quinten was found 'not guilty' of the charge. He came out of the court ecstatic and that evening he went to China Whites celebrating the result. Unbeknown to him the Sun was running the match-fixing story the next day. Someone must have rung him in the morning because the waiting paparazzi got shots of him running over to the newsagents, in pyjama bottoms and coat, to get a copy of the paper where he found himself the subject of the headlines. The World Snooker Association phoned me up and I told them that the Sun newspaper had all the evidence. Quinten was immediately suspended pending an investigation. For every hearing that was arranged where Quinten could defend himself, he submitted a doctor's note saying that he was unfit to attend. This meant that he was still getting paid his first-round prize money, even though he was not competing in the tournaments, because they were unable to discipline him legally in his absence.

Finally, Quinten was given an ultimatum to turn up at a hearing or he would be banned from the game. He turned up and was fined £20,000 and he was banned for life from playing snooker. He rang me to say that I had ruined his life. I said that he should think about the girls' lives that he has ruined over the years and that I wouldn't be surprised if one day I read in the paper that he had raped and murdered someone and buried them in his garden. I said that he needed medical help. I also said that he should have paid me my money and that when I said that he wouldn't pick up a cue again, I meant it! I hung up on him and I have never spoken to him since.

MAKING THE BREAK AND MEETING MICHAEL CARROLL

At the end of February things finally came to a head with Denise. I don't know how long I would have kept things going but I rang her one night, well in the early hours of the morning, and I was rambling drunkenly that I was not happy, and I couldn't carry on living a lie. She told me afterwards that as I put the phone down, she willed the telephone not to disconnect. I said goodnight to her, slurred incoherently that I would call her the next day, put the receiver down and then I turned to Karen and said that I wanted to wake up in the morning and see her every day, that I hated my life at home and that I was sick of living a lie. Denise, in complete shock, heart pounding, was still listening on the phone that hadn't disconnected. The game was up.

I was already living with Karen, so things didn't change for me, except that Denise knew that I had moved out. At about the same time, I had become aware of a guy by the name of Michael Carroll, not for any other reason but for the fact that he had won £9.7 million on the lottery. He lived in a place called Downham Market in Norfolk. I had already been doing quite a bit of work with the tabloid newspapers and I had some great contacts. Michael had been in trouble with the police, and he was by all accounts a rough, if not tough, cookie.

I decided to make a trip down to his neck of the woods, so Karen and I jumped in the car and headed for Norfolk. By now I had got her to give her notice in at the pub where she worked and had employed her as my PA. I had the idea that I would get Carroll into a boxing ring, where his aggression would have to be controlled and also, I thought that it would be great to be able to motivate him and get him off his path of self-destruction.

It was about a five-hour drive to get to Downham Market and when we got there, I asked a passer-by if he knew where Michael Carroll lived. He pointed me in the right direction and then, two more people later, we finally found ourselves outside his house. There were two huge lions' heads flanking the iron gate and a sign that read 'Beware of the Dog'.

From a distance the house looked impressive, a detached residence in a rural setting. On closer inspection, I could see that it was neglected and in front of the building was a car graveyard. There were about sixty vehicles strewn around the front of the property and the building itself was in a sorry state of disrepair. None of the cars looked driveable and there was a battered tow truck discarded there. Tyres littered the area, intermingled with dog faeces. Empty beer bottles punctuated what should have been a lawn and burnt areas marked long gone fires. The whole area had been churned up with obvious vehicular activity. A house that once probably echoed with the sounds of children now creaked beneath a façade of destitution, belying the wealth of its owner.

I pressed the intercom button at the gate.
"Hello!" It was a woman's voice.
"Hello, I've come to see Michael Carroll."
"Who are ya?!" she rasped
"My name's George Bamby, I'm a boxing promoter."
"Aar…eee don't live 'ere." I tried to picture the face behind the voice.
"I've driven a long way and I'd really like to see him" I continued.
"Well, I can't get in touch with him" she was irritating me by now.
"Listen" I said, "I'm going to post a DVD in the post box with my phone number. Tell Michael to have a look at it and tell him to give me a ring if he's interested. I'll be at the hotel but I'm not leaving until I've spoken to him."

I posted a copy of the DVD that I'd had made of the Hann/King fight and a note with my phone number and then Karen and I went back to the hotel. At about half two in the morning my mobile rang.
"Alright Chav, is that George? It's Michael Carroll."
Fucking hell Michael," I said, "nice to talk to you."
"What's going on?" he asked, "What's the crack?"
I said, "Well you know how you are always in trouble for fighting?"
"Err Yeah…" I could almost hear his brain ticking. "I love a bit of a fight me."
"How do you fancy getting in a ring in front of a few thousand people and having a proper fight?"
"Fucking hell, yeah…I'd love that!" It was obvious that he was excited by the prospect.
I threw wood onto his fire saying, "You can get all yer mates down to watch it and it may be on TV, you'll look brilliant."
"Oh yes!" he said.
He was hooked.
"Put me in for that, just let me know what day it is, and I'll turn up."
"It doesn't work like that" I explained raising my eyebrows at Karen "You'll have to meet me tomorrow when we can talk properly about it

and I'll have a contract ready for you to sign. If you want to do it, great, if you don't, then fine."
"Right" he said, not about to jeopardise his fifteen minutes of fame. "Come round to the house in Downham Market, tomorrow at eleven o'clock."
That was it: I had a foot in the door.

The next morning, as arranged, I turned up at the house. The gates were open, so we drove straight in, onto the remains of what was once the drive.
A big woman with an even bigger voice came out of the house.
"'Ere, Mikey's not 'ere at the moment. Don't know what time eees goin ta be 'ere. He knows ya comin…ya'll just 'ave ta wait"

We must have sat in the car for a couple of hours, but I was determined that I was not going to leave without talking to him. Suddenly a Range Rover swung into the drive, followed by a second vehicle. It was a gang about nine-strong. They had parked so that my exit route out of the property was blocked so I was a bit worried. I recognised Michael Carroll from his photographs; he was sitting in the passenger seat of the first vehicle, so I approached, smiling despite my anxiety. The window slid down a few inches and I said,
"Hi Mikey, how yer doin'? My name's George. Are you alright?"
"Yeah, chav, yeah…I'm alright."
'Chav', I would learn later is his nickname of choice for any acquaintance that he meets.
"Listen…do you want to do some boxing?" I asked straight away, after all we had been waiting hours and I wasn't going to stand around making small talk.
"Yeah…yeah…man…I fucking wanna do some boxing."
On the note that I left at his house the night before, I had asked him to bring a DVD player to the meeting.
"Right then," I went on, "we need to sit down and have a proper chat."
He replied, "Yeah, yeah, we'll talk now."
"We're not talking with all your cronies in the van." I objected.
One of his mates in the back of the van shouted, "Who you calling a fucking cronie?!"
I said, "Look Mikey, if you want to do this and you want to do it properly, we need to sit down, have a chat, and sort it out professionally."
He was looking at me blankly, so I continued,

"If you want to talk to me, then great…we'll talk one-to-one but I'm not getting involved with all your fucking mates."
Now we were both speaking the same language.
"You can talk to all of them after, if you want to, and tell them what we are going to do" I added in case he needed more convincing.
Mikey turned his head and nodded for the gang to get out. The Godfather had spoken. It's amazing how money can buy respect or feigned respect at least. The posse went over to inspect the abandoned vehicles, some of them getting in and revving engines. I climbed up into the driving seat of the car, next to Michael Carroll and I shook his hand.

He had a portable DVD player in the car, so I put on the DVD of the Hann/King fight, talking him through the details. I had four contracts prepared, one for £25,000, one for £10,000, one for £5,000 and one for nothing.
I said, "I can make you famous if that's what you want, I can get you on TV shows, I can get you a book deal…"
"That's all I wanna do" he interrupted, animated with excitement, "I wanna be famous."
"Why don't you sign me up as your agent?" I suggested.
"Yeah, yeah, yeah man" he was already swept away on the celebrity wave.
"If you want me to be your agent, I will be your agent," I said, "but it will cost you five grand as a down payment, and you will have to sign a contract."
"Yeah, yeah, yeah man" he was already picturing himself on the front page of GQ
He was now talking in a 'street' accent. It was an accent that is fine if you are actually black and it's a natural accent but coming out of the mouth of this country Norfolk boy it seemed almost pathetic. I imagined that he had never even seen a street in a tough area of London, never mind lived on one.

I put my hand up through the sunroof and gestured for Karen to bring over the contract, circling my thumb with my index finger into a zero. This meant that I didn't have to pay Michael to get into the boxing ring. He signed it and I signed a receipt to say that he had given me five thousand pounds to engage me as his agent. I said that the deal would be that any money that I made for him henceforth would be split 50:50. Then to my surprise he said that he did not want a share of any income,

that he wanted the publicity. I suppose to someone who had won £9.7m on the lottery, the sort of money that we would be bringing in from magazine stories would be insignificant.
“I don’t want any money” he said, “just get me in the papers, get me on the telly, get me books, get me everything. You keep the money if we get any.”
That was a great result for me as it meant double payday for everything that I worked on.

We chatted for a while. I think because of my background I have an ability to talk genuinely to people on all levels, so before long we were getting on like a house on fire and he had dropped his façade and his accent. Somewhere behind his exterior of bravado there is a real person, albeit a little misguided perhaps. I hoped that it wasn’t too late and that maybe I could make a difference in his life. As we got out of the car, he put an arm round my shoulder and squeezed, then shook my hand,
“You’re alright you are. We’ve had loads of fucking people round here trying to do me”.

I started to set up Michael Carroll’s first fight, but I didn’t tell him initially who his opponent would be. I introduced him to the Repton Boxing Club in London. Tony Burns, who runs the club, is very well respected in the boxing fraternity, as much for his own integrity as for his association with the Kray twins. He is an incredible character with great motivational skills, and he tells it exactly as it is. We have a mutual respect, and I knew that putting Mikey Carroll into his hands would give him at least a fighting chance, if he could apply himself and dedicate his time to the training.

I took Michael down to London and checked him into a hotel, then afterwards I took him along to the gym. Tony laid down the law, leaving Mikey in no doubt that this was a serious fight and that the training was a genuine and punishing regime. It was a challenge that I hoped that he would rise to.

Michael was bowled over with the thought of becoming famous and he said that he wanted to be in the papers every day. I asked him what sort of publicity he wanted, and he said that he didn’t care. From that minute, I sold all sorts of stories to the papers and over the next few months hardly a week went by without him being in the paper for something. There was the boxing event to publicise and then there was his incessant bad behaviour and his relationship with his neighbours. I could not imagine having to endure living next door to him and it was difficult trying to fight his corner and defend his lifestyle. At the same time having come from the background that I had, I hoped that he too could find a different direction in life that could take him away from the negative influences. After all he had millions and if you can't turn your life around with that sort of foot up the ladder then you don't deserve anyone's respect.

Mikey openly admitted that he was heavily into drugs, and cocaine was readily available at the house. I never ate or drank anything when I visited him for fear that someone would think it was funny to put something in my food or drink. Having spent almost two years of my life taking morphine after my accident, I made my mind up that I would never be dominated by a substance again and so drug-taking is not something that I would want to get into. Michael, on the other hand, snorted large quantities of white powder and when I witnessed him and his friends smoking crack, I questioned whether I wanted to be involved with him at all. If he was going to turn his life around then he would have to cut out the drink and the drugs. I was not sure that he could and on top of that I was not sure that he wanted to. I think that it was my own aspirations for him that kept me involved; I kept thinking that there was so much that he could do with his life with all the money that he had. Michael just seemed intent on self-destruction and was happy to throw his life away.

A training schedule at the boxing club had been worked out for him to ensure that he would be in some sort of shape for the fight, but right from the beginning he was only turning up to one session in four. He had already told all his mates that he was boxing so maybe he thought that it would damage their 'respect' for him if he withdrew from the fight. The consensus of opinion in his hometown seemed to be that the majority hoped that he would be defeated and that they would enjoy someone else doing for them what many would have liked to do themselves!

I organised interviews where Michael never even bothered to show up. One morning I sat alone on the couch of TVAM making excuses for him and defending his behaviour. At that moment I could happily have walked away but by that time I had made commitments with regard to the boxing event and cancellation was not an option.

I was pleased when Mark Smith, famously the persona behind 'Rhino', one of the Gladiators, agreed to be the opponent that would face Michael Carroll in the ring. Mikey was not overly keen!
"A gladiator?..I'm not fighting a fucking gladiator!"

In a packed arena, at Bethnel Green in London, he did fight a gladiator. The outcome was inevitable, and the crowd cheered like Roman spectators baying for the blood of a condemned criminal. Mikey's girlfriend, Sammy, also had her own melee in the crowd which escalated into a brawl involving about fifty people.

After the fight, I upped Mikey's profile with a continued programme of publicity, aiming to fulfil his ambition to become famous. My agenda was to make him a household name. By now I had resigned myself to the fact that he was happy with his life as it was and that our arrangement was going to be short term. Unless he was going to make lifestyle changes then his shelf-life as a public commodity was limited. The last thing that I would do for him would be to arrange a biographer to write his story. I recruited a man from London and introduced him with a view to him ghost-writing Michael's autobiography. He turned out to be another of life's cuckoos: that wait until someone else has built the nest and then they steal the eggs. The arrangement was that the writer would be paid a fee of £5,000 to write the book after which he would have no further involvement.

Unexpectedly then, Mikey rang me to say that he wanted a rematch with Rhino! I was shocked to receive the call but started making arrangements the minute we finished talking. He told me that he wanted to pay Rhino to let him win though this time, but I said that I couldn't get involved with anything like that. I think that he was determined that he would redeem himself in the eyes of his peers and whatever it took, he wanted to win.

The fight was arranged for the MEN arena in Manchester. This was against my better judgement as I considered the venue too big and the overheads were immense, but I had a partner involved who was adamant that we put on an impressive event.
On the same bill, we had Jodie Marsh fighting Lindsey Dawn Mckensie, John Adridge (former Liverpool and R.O.I. centre forward) fighting Clayton Blackmore (ex Man Utd player), Craig Phillips (Big Brother)

fighting Teddy Gibson (ex Man Utd.). The main bout was Michael Carroll against Mark Smith aka 'Rhino'…the rematch!

Leading up to the event, Mikey didn't train, he didn't turn up for interviews even though he swore that he would, and I knew that our days together were numbered. Michael had no respect for himself or anyone else. On the day of the fight, Mark Smith phoned me and said that Mikey had given him twenty grand and asked him to let him win, which I guessed explained why Mikey felt that he didn't need to train. There was no way that Mark would throw the fight.

As I walked into the dressing room where Mikey was getting ready for the bout, he was taking a line of 'coke' and there were six empty Stella bottles on the table.
"That's it, Mikey!" I screamed, "You are not fucking fighting! You are not getting in the ring….I am pulling the fucking plug. Get in your car and fuck off!"
"I've gotta fight" he retaliated, "I'm the main fighter!"
"Mikey! I am not going to be responsible for you getting in the ring with six cans of Stella and a couple of lines of coke inside you! What if something happens?"
"It won't! It won't!...I've given him twenty grand, he's going to go easy on me!"
I got Rhino in, and I said that Mikey been drinking and taking coke and now we were in a bloody awful position.

Five minutes later they were in the ring and Rhino gave Mikey Carroll the pasting of his life.

The next morning Mikey rang me,
"George!" he said but it didn't sound like him, the voice was nasal and muffled.
"What are you sounding like that for?" I asked him.
"My nose got broke last night," he went on, "and me cheek bone!"
I feigned sympathy but really by then I couldn't care less as he had let me down badly and I felt that he deserved what he got.

The biographer, Shaun Boru, moved in with Mikey for a week and promptly set about annihilating the relationship that we had. He said that I was taking advantage of him by taking the money for newspaper stories, even though that was the agreement that we had made. I was not being paid a retainer by Mikey to represent him and on top of that we had lost money on the last fight. I have seen it many times before, when people see what they think is an opportunity to make money and then they make all sorts of promises that they can't keep. Michael Carroll and I severed our connections. Sean Boru wrote his autobiography, and not surprisingly tried to jump into my shoes as his manager, but by the time the book was published Mikey had sunk back into insignificance. He no longer had me working on his behalf to keep him in the news. There was one copy of the book in our local bookshop, and at the time of writing it is still there!

For the whole time that I was involved with Michael Caroll, I was with Karen. We must have been together for almost a year and a half, but during that time I left and went back to Denise at least a dozen times. When I was with Karen, I wanted to be with Denise and Lewis and then as soon as I went back, I wanted to be with Karen again. I would throw my things back into the car and head back up the M5 and then as soon as I got back to Karen, I thought that I had made a mistake. I don't know why they both put up with so much from me. Karen was by far the more volatile: I drove her into fits of rage. Once as I left, she threw a tub of 'I don't believe it's not Butter' down the road after me, shouting.
"I don't even fucking like that, you can take it with you!"

At one point, I had clothes in both houses and they both thought that I was living with them. I think Denise took me back so many times because of Lewis. She protected him from everything that went on and when I asked her to, she even booked a caravan where Karen and I could stay in Devon. Later she said it was because she wanted Lewis to be able to see his dad, even just for a few days. Now I realise how hard it must have been for her. As it happened, during that holiday, I had a huge row with Karen, and we left in a hurry. Much to Denise's disgust I dropped Lewis back early and then had the cheek to ring her when I hit the motorway and realised that I had left a couple of grand in cash in the one of the cupboards at thc caravan! I asked her to pick it up before she dropped the keys back to the owner. When she went, she found that Karen had also left a wardrobe full of clothes there, so she retrieved those too. I am a nightmare!

During this time, Graham from the Child Protection Unit in Manchester went to Devon to take a statement from Denise, in relation to my historical case. She told him that she didn't owe me anything but, as she had said that she would give a statement, she would tell him what she heard when I made the phone call to my stepdad from Gibraltar. Graham jokingly told her that if he had known what he was letting himself in for when he took the case on, he would not have answered the phone that day. He also told her that it's almost as if I have a self-destruct button, that when at last I have got something good, then I have to mess things up. They talked for hours, and Graham knew that she was telling the truth. She believed my story and the phone call, between me and my stepdad, had been evidence enough to convince her.

Whilst I was living with Karen I didn't see as much of Lewis as I should have done but I made the excuses to myself that I was busy with work but when I wasn't working, I took Karen away for long weekends and we went abroad every few months. As I was still paying the mortgage and maintaining her and Lewis, I didn't think Denise had anything to moan about. When I didn't turn up for his sports day when I said I would, I think she made her mind up to move on. She took Lewis over on holiday to Gibraltar with a view to them moving back there as she had been offered a job running a restaurant for some old friends of hers. I rang her and said that I was coming home to my family and would be waiting for them when they got back, but before she had even got off the plane I was already back in Cheshire with Karen.

Denise didn't leave though but instead she waited, and waited, and then one day I realised that I was losing the best thing that had ever happened to me and for what? I packed up my stuff for the last time and I went home. Things weren't easy when I first got back but this time, I was determined to work things out.

ARREST

Graham and I had many a long conversation on the phone and I had been into the office a few times. He had been to see Vicky and at first, he thought she was going to come through for me, but then she decided that she didn't want to make a statement. She had, though, already admitted to Graham that what I had told him was the truth. Graham tried but could not convince her to take the stand and so we had to resign ourselves to the fact that the only person that could corroborate any of my story was Denise.

On top of that, the police were having problems finding out where my mum and stepdad were living. I rang Dave, my cousin, who refused to tell me, but he gave me an idea of where it was. I spent hours driving around Manchester in the areas that I thought they lived. One day I saw Kelly coming out of a house and I did not go unspotted. I didn't care as I had the address at last and Graham and the Child Protection Unit could make their next move.

A couple of days later there was a knock at the door, at home in Devon. It was two policemen, one of whom asked if I was George Bamby. I invited them in, and I was served with a 'Notice of Unwanted Contact' and asked to keep away from my family. Kelly had apparently started training in the police force and had instigated an injunction. I explained the situation to the two officers and gave the contact details for the Child Protection Unit. I said that I had no further need to be in the vicinity of my family now, that I was just trying to find out where they lived, as the police had exhausted their search.

A few weeks later, Graham rang me to say that my mother and stepdad had been arrested and taken to the station where they had been questioned. I made him go over and over it, repeating every detail of what had happened, who said what and how they had reacted. It was hard to believe that it was really happening. They were released on bail to appear in the local magistrates' court in six months' time.

PAPPARAZZI

Back in Devon, I had to earn a living. I had fallen out with Michael Carroll, and I needed something to motivate and stimulate me. Having been involved for so long with the tabloid newspapers, I knew what sorts of stories made sales and I knew what made money. I pondered long and hard on what made the paparazzi tick, how did they get their pictures, did they have a conscience? In a single moment I had it! I was going to become a paparazzo photographer and I would live, eat and breathe their lives and then I was going to write a book about them or maybe even a sitcom.

What happened next was quite unexpected. I did become a photographer, but I was so good at it that within months I was one of the most successful paparazzi photographers in the UK! I bought a camera on eBay and then a couple of lenses and I set to work, knowing absolutely nothing about photography!

For the first couple of months, I got many shots that were out of focus and the staff at Big Pictures in London apparently cheered when I sent through my first in-focus photograph. I soon mastered the art of the camera and although I knew that I would not make a David Bailey, I had the ability to get the picture and that was worth far more than creativity. I loved the challenge and the thrill of the work, but I always kept a respectable distance from my celebrity friends unless invited.

I went over to Germany for the World Cup 2006 and in the pre-match training sessions in Portugal, I got some of the most published photographs of all the 'snappers' there. I got more shots than any of the professionals, but it was not without its dangers as I had to run away on a few occasions from the Portuguese police.

In Germany, I accompanied David Beckham's mum to the park with her grandchildren and the minders. I took some wonderful shots of the boys which I gave to Mrs. Beckham in an album. Those shots were not for sale but in return Victoria posed for me with some supporters and I made a killing with a great shot of her in shorts which appeared in all the UK magazines and newspapers. In Germany, the press thought I was such a character that they asked me to appear in a television documentary and one of the German magazines did a double page article about me!

BACK TO REALITY

Michael Carroll had been in prison for months, convicted of an assault charge, and before our argument he had given me some money to buy some celebrity memorabilia. I had bought it but it was stored in my office at home so I was glad when he rang to say that he was out, and I could finally get it out of the way. He asked me to bring it round and said that we may be able to do a few more things together.

I decided to keep an open mind, but Denise didn't want me to get involved with him again. I insisted and said that at least I wanted to take him the stuff that I had bought on his behalf. So, I drove all the way over to Norfolk and went to his Auntie Kelly's house, who assured me that Mikey was a reformed character. I rang Denise and said that I had a funny feeling about this meeting, and she was adamant that I should go with my gut instinct and come back home straight away.
"If it doesn't feel right, then it probably isn't" she said wisely.
She asked me to just drop the stuff off somewhere where he could pick it up. In hindsight, very foolishly I drove to Michael's Auntie Kelly's house, as arranged.

Michael was nowhere to be seen, so I unloaded the car and took all the framed pictures into the house. Then Mikey phoned me and asked me to wait there but I still had a nagging feeling of apprehension, so I went outside and sat in the car. It wasn't long before Michael turned up and I saw him go in and then, through the window, I saw him go into the kitchen where Kelly poured them both a drink. She came out to the front door with her boyfriend and stood on the step. Still, I sat in the car. Kelly came over and knocked on the window.
"Mikey's in there" she said helpfully, "why don't you go and have a chat with him now?"
I got out of the car and went into the house.

"Hi Mikey, there's all your memorabilia." I said, indicating where I had stacked everything against the wall.
"Never mind the memorabilia, what about the twenty grand that you and Rhino took off me?"
"What d'ya mean?... What twenty grand that me and Rhino took off you?" I asked in disbelief
"That twenty grand that I gave him to throw the fight, when he didn't throw the fight, he beat the shit out of me, and you and him had the fucking twenty grand between you"

"I didn't have a penny out of that!...It was nothing to do with me!" I replied to deaf ears.
"Yer a fucking liar!" he said, turning to lock the back door to the kitchen. Past the front window I saw four youths on their way in. As I turned to look, Michael swung a punch, hitting the side of my jaw and throwing me violently back against the cooker. I was off balance and before I knew what was happening, I was being punched and kicked from every direction, all five of them beating me to the ground and into unconsciousness.

I came round in a pool of blood, the group of them sitting at the table, laughing, the remains of a bottle of vodka in the middle of them. I dragged myself up onto my knees and then pulled one leg up to stand. As I did so, the smallest of the group stood up and swung another punch at me. My survival instinct leapt into action, and I smacked him as hard as I could, the adrenaline surging through my body giving me the strength to stand up and run for the front door which was ajar. I had left the car unlocked, probably because I was feeling so anxious, so I threw myself into the passenger seat and pressed the button to centrally lock the vehicle. Jumping over into the driving seat, I fumbled to get my key into the ignition. Faces surrounded me and one of the youths had climbed onto the bonnet. I accelerated away sending him spinning onto the road and I drove away at breakneck speed, not stopping until I was sure that I was not being followed.

I pulled down the sun visor and inspected my face in the mirror. It was already swelling and bruising, I had a vicious cut above one eye and my mouth and teeth were bleeding. My face and shirt were both covered in blood. I rang Denise. She had been trying to ring me for the past hour and was frantic with worry, every intuitive nerve in her body telling her that something was wrong. She was about to ring the police when I rang her. I told her what had happened, and she was upset and angry and said that I should drive straight away to the nearest police station.
"Sweetheart, I'm coming home," I said.
She begged me not to drive all the way home in that state and said that I should check into a hotel for the night and drive back in the morning.

I was in shock and was not to be reasoned with, so I drove from Norfolk to Devon, stopping only once for petrol when it was not possible to drive any further. I walked into the service station looking like something

from the Living Dead. The lad on the counter must have wondered what on earth had happened to me.
"Are you alright, mate?" he asked.
"Yes" I said though I plainly was not.
I decided not to press charges even though Denise wanted me to. I didn't want to get involved in a court case and I know what goes around comes around. One day Michael Carroll will cross someone else, and he will deserve everything that he gets.

THE ACCUSEDS' PLEA

The date eventually came when my mum and stepdad appeared in the Magistrate's court. Graham, true to his word, kept me informed throughout the process so I knew that they would be bailed again to appear at the County Court. This went on for months. They had pleaded 'Not Guilty' to all eleven charges, so time had to be given to all the barristers concerned to compile and collate evidence.

The case was referred to the Crown Prosecution Service who had to decide whether they wanted to take the case to trial. Graham was elated when he rang me to say that the CPS were behind us wholeheartedly and that after reading all the evidence they wanted Carole and Arthur Cooper in court facing the charges.

For months I kept busy taking photographs and at the same time working on the beginnings of a storyline based on the paparazzi. I got some brilliant stuff and Denise started to make up folders of my work for reference. Unfortunately, I lost a few celebrity friends when they found out that I was involved with the press. I didn't want to tell anyone that I was doing research as I had been accepted into the paparazzi fraternity. I was earning a good living at the same time, and it was a fantastic experience that challenged and tested me every day that I did the job. I knew that my real friends would still be there and some like Mike le Velle stood by me, even though others were slagging me off. I didn't want to compromise anyone, so I kept out of the way for a few months, meeting up with close mates when I was in the Manchester area and giving myself the opportunity to make new friends in Devon and to finally settle into a home life with Denise and Lewis.

One morning, I woke up to the sound of the post landing on the doormat. There were two similar letters, one addressed to me and the other to Denise. It was the details and confirmation of the court date.

THE COURT CASE

The day before the case, Denise and I had confirmation of the hotel where we would be staying in Manchester, and we made arrangements to meet someone from the witness service so that we could go into the court before the hearing.

We drove up the M5, both of us tense with nerves, and as we neared the centre of Manchester, I could feel the hollowness of my stomach as I struggled to maintain my composure.
"Let's not go to the court now, let's just go in the morning." I suggested to Denise.
"That woman, Rachel, will be waiting for us. Come on, please let's go, it will make me feel better if we can go into the courtroom before the morning. I am having panic attacks I am so nervous….and it will be good for you to have a look at the court before we have to go in." Denise replied convincingly.
I wanted to turn the car around, drive straight back to Devon and forget about the whole thing, but it was too late
A couple of wrong turns then suddenly there it was, a huge building commanding respect, holding its own court.

We pulled into the car park across the road, as near to the building as we could. I looked at Denise and I could see that she was nervous, her left hand clutched desperately at her right thumb.
"There!" she said, pointing to a door away from the main entrance, at the side of the building. "That's the door! Ring her and tell her we are here."
We were half an hour late, but it was because of a reluctance to get there.
"There!" Denise said as the door opened, "That must be her, standing at the door!"

We jumped out of the car and walked over to the woman standing in the doorway.
"George?" she offered an outstretched hand.
I shook it. "Pleased to meet you, Rachel, sorry we are so late, this is Denise."
"Hello Denise," she offered her hand in greeting. "Don't worry, you are here now, let's get inside"
She led the way into the corridor where a policeman manned a metal detector.

"Can you put your keys and phone in the basket please sir, and walk through?"
The security was reassuring but at the same time intimidating.
"This whole area is the Witness Protection Suite which is situated under the Courts. You can go into a communal room if you wish but we have put aside a room for your sole use during the case".

Rachel showed us the 'smoking room' where I joked that I would be spending the duration of my time. We then saw the communal area where people were sitting quietly with serious faces. Denise was silent and as I squeezed her hand, I could feel the tension in her body. Rachel showed us the room where we would be expected to wait before we gave evidence, then she led us through a maze of corridors which came out into Court no. 6.

One of the original Victorian courts, No. 6 was newly renovated and given a new lease of life, but the room echoes with the years of judicial protocol. The wood has absorbed the sweat of hundreds of palms, clutching onto the belief that justice would be done. The gallery, only almost above shoulder height from where onlookers would have heckled the proceedings, now lay empty. Our footsteps reverberated and as I took a step up into the witness box, I felt sick in the very pit of my stomach. Denise took her turn up in the box. She looked like a small girl on her first day at school and clutching her hands over her mouth, she exhaled loudly.
"The room is smaller than I expected" she said trying to smile at me. "I'm glad we came in, aren't you?"
Denise asked if she could practice the oath. She was as nervous about speaking in public as she was about giving evidence. That was not something that had not even entered my head and I found it hard to empathise with the fear that she was feeling.
"I hate to hear the sound of my voice….everyone listening…I would give anything not to have to do this," she said, and then read out the oath from the card.
I knew that Denise was putting herself through this ordeal for me and I felt almost humbled. She hates being in the spotlight, but because she knew that she was the main witness, she was prepared to stand up on my behalf.

We looked at the dock where my mother and stepfather would be sitting behind glass; we saw where the barristers would sit and the clerk to the court.
"The jury are so close to us, aren't they?" Denise said in a half-whisper. Three tiered benches faced the witness box.
"When the barristers question you, you must direct your answers to the jury… They are the ones that you are talking to." The Clerk to the Court had come in and offered advice.
"That seat over there is where the person from the Witness Service will sit. They will be with you the whole time and escort you to and from the court…and I will be here if you should need a drink of water, I am just here," he indicated where he would be located.
"Are you ready? Shall we go back down?" Rachel asked.

We left shortly afterwards and went to check in at the hotel. Neither Denise nor I could eat anything that night. We ordered Room Service, but our appetites had deserted us. The room and the bed were unfamiliar, and Denise never sleeps well in strange beds. We whispered to each other in the dark of the room and just when sleep finally crept upon us, we were woken by the sound of dripping water. There was a leak in the ceiling and the only remedy was to throw towels to muffle the sound of the incessant dripping. In the early hours, I gave up trying to sleep and went down and sat for hours in reception, having coffee and making idle conversation with the staff.

We ordered breakfast in our room which neither of us could eat and then, like condemned prisoners, we knew that the time had finally come when we could no longer put off leaving. We had to go to court. The day had arrived.
I had paid for a private bodyguard, and he was waiting for us in the hotel reception. Denise and I sat silent in the back of his car and then as we drove to the court, I filled him in on a bit of background information about the case.

Denise said that she had never felt so nervous in her entire life. I felt sick. As we drove up and I saw the building looming ahead I felt like that first day at the children's home when we drove up the drive, not knowing what to expect. We parked on the same car park, as close to the side door as we could, and Richard, the bodyguard, got out first and after looking around he nodded that we should get out. The air was crisp and cool, a bright and sunny September morning. It felt much earlier than the actual time of 8.30am, probably because my eyes were stinging from lack of sleep, but by now the adrenaline was pumping to every cell in my body.

We went through the detector and along the corridor to our allocated room. One of the Witness Service volunteers came in and introduced herself. Maureen was calm and quietly spoken and she talked to us like she had known us for years. She said that she would not leave my side until I left the building. She was probably in her sixties, slightly built and not much taller than five feet but she had a huge personality and she put me at ease. Maureen got both Denise and I a coffee and we sat with Richard. It was like waiting to go in for an operation. Maureen asked if we wanted to watch a DVD and so we put on Phoenix Nights to try and take our minds off the proceedings.

A short while later, Graham came in, smartly dressed in suit and tie. We shook hands.
"Well mate, this is it!" he said "Your barrister will be in shortly and you will be given your statements to read before you give evidence. Maurice Green is one of the best."
To one side, he asked why I felt that I needed a bodyguard. I explained that my brother's gym is in that area and that I didn't want to take any unnecessary risks coming in and leaving the court with Denise. Graham went out and came back in a couple of minutes later to say that I would be given an armed police guard to take me up into the courtroom. Rachel then came in and said that I had been given a special dispensation to allow me to enter the court through the judges' chambers. That apparently was unheard of. I was relieved that I would not have to walk through the public areas, which was one less thing to worry about.

Soon afterwards, my barrister came in and gave me my statement to read. He said that I would have to read it alone somewhere and that once I had read it and given it back, I would not be permitted to see it again. I didn't need to read it as I knew exactly what was in it. I knew that there was nothing that the defence barristers could catch me out on as I had only said the truth. As instructed, I went to the smokers' room and read through my statement. Graham came in and wished me luck and said that we would not be allowed to see each other again until after he had given his evidence. Back in the waiting room Denise was looking tense, pacing the floor.

"Are you ok darling?" she asked as I walked back in.
"Yeah, just dreading seeing those two fuckers when I get up there…but at the same time I can't wait to see them."

There was a knock at the door and three people from the Crown Prosecution Service came in and introduced themselves. I was too nervous to take it all in at the time, but apparently the woman who came in was the person who had been insistent that they take the case on. I wish that I could have thanked her. I don't even remember talking to them. The young man with her was going to be in the court representing the CPS. He was confident and friendly, and I felt overwhelmed that for once people were with me in my corner. No-one there was calling me a liar or an attention seeker. They had studied the case, everything, barristers had made assessments and finally after almost a year and a half we were there: team Bamby.

Suddenly the door opened. Maureen held it open and smiled.
"They are ready for you."
Denise said that I walked out of the room in a trance, that I didn't even look round at anyone. It was all that I could do to put one foot in front of the other. Outside, a uniformed policeman was waiting, and he escorted me through the corridors. *Walking.*
Step…step…step..step…
Door…
Step..
My throat was dry, and my heart was pounding. The policeman talked to me as we went up through the building. I know that they were words of encouragement but the blood pumping in my ears kept the sound out.

Then I was in the court. I looked ahead, focussing on the wooden frame of the witness box. The room was silent except for the whispering of papers.

Where were they?
There, behind the glass. Both looking ahead. Not looking at me.
Why aren't they looking at me?
Can he feel my eyes burning into his face?
No, he's still looking ahead.
They look older. My stepdad looks fat in his white shirt, his robe of respectability. My mother still has her hair bleached. She looks stern with an unforgiving mouth, a mouth that has uttered so many

obscenities, smoked so many cigarettes. There were never any kisses hiding in the corner of that mouth.

I looked away and then took a second to look at the jury, nodding my head in silent greeting.
Twelve Good Men.
So, these were the people that were to decide the outcome. I looked from face to face.
All of them, staring at me.

I had decided the day before that I would sit in the witness box rather than stand. This position would prevent any direct eye contact with my mother and stepdad.
After swearing my oath on the bible, my barrister stood and said that he wanted to take me through my statement. I gave evidence for the whole day. It was exhausting. I had to relive each incident from my childhood, in detail, sharing with complete strangers my innermost feelings, opening boxes that I had stuffed to the darkest recesses in my mind. I was emotional and at times it was hard to retain my composure. Often, I would feel anger welling up inside as I talked about the abuse that I had suffered. I still couldn't unburden the overwhelming feeling of injustice I carried with me, because everyone as a child said that I was a liar and an attention seeker.

This time it was my turn to be heard. My stepfather could no longer punch and smack me, he had to sit in silence and hear the catalogue of abuse that I endured at his hands. I was asked about the shooting incident, the chilli incident, the rice pudding incident, the charity box incident. I was asked to talk about defecating in my room and my false imprisonment. I explained to the jury that at one point I had felt so bad that I wanted to kill myself and said as much to my stepdad. He went into the kitchen and came back with a bottle of tablets. He had sent Vicky and Kelly to bed already and he banged the container down on the table in front of me.
"There you go then," he said, "fucking kill yerself.....go on...fucking take them!"
When I said that I didn't want to, he said that either I took them, or he was going to give me another battering. Either way I was taking them. My mother sat at his side, both of them laughing. He took the top from the container and emptied the small white tablets onto the table.
"Go on then, if yer want to fucking kill yerself"

Sobbing, I picked up tablet after tablet and swallowed them with sips of water from the glass that Arthur had provided. I took them all.
My mother and stepfather were laughing.
"Don't worry, it will be just like going to sleep" he said
"Yeah, except you wont fucking wake up" my mother added, and they cackled in unison.
"Get to bed!" my stepdad ordered.
I cried myself to sleep. I didn't want to die. Surely I had a life to live didn't I?
Was this it? I was never going to be a professional footballer. I was going to die instead, and they were both going to be happy.
The next morning, I was still alive. I woke up. Why wasn't I dead?
My mother took the chain off the door and popped her head into my room.
"Yer soft fucker! D'ya think we would give you tablets?" and she laughed, returning to her bedroom to share the joke with my stepfather.
Apparently, they had given me antibiotics or some other prescribed medicine but not ones that would kill me.

As I finished relating this incident I looked towards the jury. I could see a woman on the front row fighting back tears and I felt a lump rising in my throat. It wasn't right what they did to me. Not by any stretch of the imagination, in no way would any of these people think that they were just having a laugh.

I was ready for the cross examination. I had no fear of tripping myself up. I said to Denise that as long as I stuck to the truth then there was no way that they could trick me into saying anything that would discredit my version of events. One of the defence lawyers made the mistake of calling Arthur Cooper my father. I stopped him abruptly and corrected him, asking him not to refer to him as my father. I had an answer for every question that they asked. When my stepdad's barrister reached the part in my statement when I talked about the telephone conversation, he suggested that instead of saying "We were just having a laugh," that in fact he had said, "We had some laughs". The two things have opposing meanings and I knew exactly what he had said. There was, and still is, no doubt in my mind. Denise heard him say it and we talked about it afterwards, the next day and in the months and years that followed. It was not something that either of us were going to forget. When I asked my stepdad why he did those things to me as a child, why he shot me with an air rifle, why he made me eat dog meat sandwiches, he replied,

"George, we were just having a laugh."

I maintained my composure well but when a statement was read out by Maurice Green, the barrister, made by my mother to social services when I was in hospital, I felt as if someone had stabbed me through the heart. When asked why she had not visited me, she said…and it was quoted in court,
"I hated him from the minute that he was born, and I have hated him every day since."
Even though I knew that she didn't intend me to hear it, those words, so plainly stated were extremely hard to take and I cried.

I gave evidence for the whole day and then Denise and I went back to the hotel. We were under strict instructions not to talk about the case and neither of us wanted to jeopardise the proceedings, so we kept off the subject. We were both shattered and got into bed early. Denise asked me how things had gone but I didn't even want to talk about that. We rang Lewis who was at home being taken care of by his grandad, Denise's father, and 'Auntie' Paula. Denise had left lists of instructions and a week's worth of ironed school uniforms. Lewis was happy and we knew that he was in safe hands.

The next morning, we were back in court. Denise was even more nervous as she knew that today could be the day that she had to go into the witness box.

At half eleven in the morning, they had finished with me, and Denise was summoned. She says that it was one of the worst experiences of her life. Afterwards she told me how it went. She explained how neither my mother or stepfather looked at her at all as she went in or for the entire time that my barrister was going over her statement. He only talked to her about the telephone conversation and when she repeated that Arthur had said they were 'having a laugh', Maurice Green asked her what my reaction was. She answered saying that I'd said that I was just a boy, that it wasn't a laugh and then, with emotion building, she turned to face the defendants in the dock and shouted out,
"He was a boy! You were supposed to be looking after him!"

Their barristers tried once more to say that we had misquoted the telephone conversation, but Denise would not be swayed. She was concerned though that they had planted a doubt in the jury's mind as she couldn't remember anything else about the conversation. The barrister kept saying that it was convenient, leading the jury to draw their own conclusions. Maurice Green asked why she could only remember that part and Denise replied that it was because she was shocked by what my stepdad said and that it was something that would stay with her forever.

When she came back downstairs from the courtroom, I was in the waiting room. Maureen said that she had shouted at my mum and stepdad and we both shed a few tears. I was so proud of her. She was relieved that her part of the ordeal was over.

We left the court straight away and headed back to Devon soon afterwards. We didn't want to stay around whilst other evidence was being heard and Graham promised to keep us informed every step of the way, with every development.
Graham gave evidence to say that he had visited Vicky at home where she had told him that I had been abused but that she wasn't prepared to give a statement. This contradicted Vicky's evidence in which she swore on oath that I was not abused. Kelly also denied that I had been abused. My mother was, according to people in the court, very cold and they said that my stepdad was "dismissive".

Finally, after the summing up by all three barristers, the jury retired to the chambers. They were deliberating for three days, three whole days! After the first day, I was frantic. Denise and I talked about nothing else. We knew that it was not cut and dried, they were not just going to be found 'not guilty' or a decision would have come back in a few hours. There were obviously some very deep discussions going on.

Graham had left me under no illusions that it was not an easy case to try. He said from the beginning that we were swimming upstream, we had no evidence and in reality, it was my word against theirs.

THE VERDICT
My mobile rang. The jury were back in. They had not reached a unanimous verdict on any of the charges! The judge had agreed to accept a majority verdict: 'Not guilty' on six charges and there was a hung jury on the other five charges. I can't say that I was surprised, but I was disappointed. I suppose that I had hoped for some miracle, hoped that they would be held accountable.

Graham spoke to me at length, telling me about CPS expectations of the case. Then he told me that before my mother and stepdad had been released from the dock, the judge had made a statement saying that they were not leaving his court vindicated of the charges, that members of the jury had wanted to find them guilty of **all** the charges and that the household that I had been brought up in was far from happy. Graham said that they did not leave the court cheering, that they knew that they had been lucky. He also said that one of the jury members was distraught with the outcome and wanted to contact me. Obviously, he could not pass on any details. That information from Graham gave me a lot of comfort and I felt like taking them to court had been worth it.

It took a while for the verdict to sink in and I had already told Graham that I didn't want the five charges for which there was hung jury, retrying. I had had my day in court and now I felt that I could really move on. I did feel that a weight had been lifted from my shoulders, especially when I got a phone call from my cousin Dave saying that my Auntie Shirley believed me now. She is not a stupid woman and the whole family knew how long the jury had been out deliberating.

After about a week I got up one morning and I said to Denise,
"Do you know what I am going to do?"
"No, George, what are you going to do?"
"I am going to make a film"
"What about?"
"I'm going to make a film about those two bastards!"
Denise laughed because she knew that I would do it.

Within three months of having the idea, I had written the script, cast the actors, found the locations and a production company, raised the funding, and started filming.

About four months after the trial, I received an email from one of the jurors. She had tracked me down from a website that I had set up about my forthcoming movie production.

Dear George,

I'm not sure how ethical this is, but I'm doing it anyway. I was on the jury of your case against your Mother and step-father and it has haunted me ever since. Every now and again I check the internet to see if your site appears. When I saw that you are, indeed, making a film of events, I felt the need to contact you to explain how it happened that your 'parents' could get away with what they had done.

From the outset, the jury seemed to be split between people who were willing to believe you outright, people who wanted to believe you but were desperate for some kind of evidence and two people who were never going to return a guilty verdict-unfortunately, one of the latter was a nurse who was involved with child protection who insisted on attempting to sway the unsure people by making a big deal of what she did for a living and declaring that your mother had always taken appropriate steps eg. in asking for intervention by social services when she felt she couldn't cope. This was despite there also being a jury member who was a children's social worker-a much more relevant profession- who initially tried to not use her job to sway the opinion of others, but ultimately had to offer her professional viewpoint, if only to give a more balanced viewpoint to people who were beginning to be swayed by the nurse.

I suppose in any group of 12 people you will always get dominant people and those who are easily led. Myself and the social worker knew from the outset that they were guilty, and nothing anyone said was ever going to change our opinion. The major problem in the case was the lack of evidence-but as I repeatedly asked the other jurors, how does anybody get convicted of anything from 20 or 30 years ago-as frequently does happen in abuse cases-if you are going to insist on hard concrete evidence?

The other major problem was the wording of the charges. If there had been a general abuse charge, I think you definitely would have managed to get a conviction. I think everybody (even the awkward two) believed that it was a violent household, but many were unwilling to give a guilty verdict on such particular events. A common statement was "I believe that he was hit but I've not been convinced by the evidence that he was 'punched and kicked'". Even the charges relating to the shot gun and the dogs, I suppose many of them thought "if he was really injured he would have needed hospital treatment" but in my opinion it was the fear you would have felt as a 7/8 year old that was more important than the actual injury.

What was particularly annoying was this ridiculous business of your mother admitting she'd said certain things, and then denying she'd said other things that were part of the same conversation. We even saw something that referred to her being charged with intimidating witnesses, yet this just made some of the jurors scared rather than wondering why an innocent person would intimidate witnesses. A couple of evenings we all left the same time as your family, and all the jurors were annoyed that we ended up bumping into them-I thought "why are you scared of them, according to you lot they're just a normal family?"

Initially, the nurse and some of the ones insisting on concrete evidence had swayed the majority of the jury so that it was basically 10 saying not guilty and 2 (myself and the social worker being the two) saying guilty. Eventually, after days of arguing, emotional blackmail and any other method, we managed to get the 'floaters' onto our side for some of the charges, which meant that for around half the charges the jury was completely split.

I would like to think that there was a re-trial or private prosecution for the charges that we could not agree on. It was obvious in my mind how you were unable to get anybody to give evidence to back up your side of the story-you may be living away now, but I suppose it takes a very strong, forthright person to tell the truth if they are still living in the area and still having to face the people involved. This case left me with very little faith in the British justice system-the people on the jury, in my opinion, all knew your parents were abusive and violent. They didn't seem to understand that in the absence of any other evidence, your testimony was evidence enough. Countless times in our arguments we reminded the others that the judge had said "you can choose to believe George" but there were 5 or 6 members who were never going to do so without more evidence.

I have a 7 year old son myself and to think that a Mother could bring somebody into her children's lives who could treat them in this way makes me so angry. As we left the jury room to return our verdicts I told the rest of the jury that I didn't know how they would be able to sleep at night, knowing they had a chance to make a difference in the fight against child abuse yet choosing not to.

I suppose the fact that you are filming this means that you have chosen not to pursue a further case. I hope this isn't the case and that you somehow manage to get somebody to back up your story, or find some kind of concrete evidence. I think that any other 12 people would have found them guilty on most of the charges, you were just unlucky with the spineless bunch that you got.

I hope that making this film gives you the closure that you need and that your own son reminds you of how precious our children are. More than anything I hope that Carol and Arthur get what they deserve and I wish that I could have done more to ensure that they did.

Yours

*E****** Q****** (name withheld)*

I did write that movie script and "STEPDAD" was made, with some celebrity names in it too. It is available on Amazon Prime. Sadly, I don't retain the rights to it and have never made any money out of it. It stars Mark Moraghan as my stepdad, and he played the part brilliantly. It was produced on a shoestring budget.

I don't know what the future will hold, but I am sure that it will be as exciting and eventful as my life so far. I have written two further scripts, fictional though, and I plan to enjoy every minute of whatever lies ahead.

When he is old enough and he reads this, my story, I want to say to him:

"Lewis George Bamby, my son, this book is for you."

THE END…BUT NOT THE END.
This is the life story of George Bamby up to 2007… to be continued….

FURTHER READING
"Confessions of the Paparazzi" by George Bamby
and Madison Webbe is available in hardback on Amazon
'Stepdad' the movie is available on Amazon Prime

Printed in Great Britain
by Amazon